YOU AND YOUR DISABLED CHILD

Revised edition, published 2010

First published in 2008 by

WOODFIELD PUBLISHING LTD
Bognor Regis ~ West Sussex ~ England ~ PO21 5EL
www.woodfieldpublishing.com

ISBN 1-84683-067-2

You and Your Disabled Child

A Practical Guide for Parents

M ARGARET B ARRETT

Woodfield

Woodfield Publishing Ltd

Woodfield House ~ Babsham Lane ~ Bognor Regis ~ West Sussex ~ PO21 5EL
telephone 01243 821234 ~ **e-mail** enquiries@woodfieldpublishing.co.uk

Interesting and informative books on a variety of subjects

For full details of all our published titles, visit our website at
www.woodfieldpublishing.co.uk

This book is dedicated to the courageous little souls from throughout the world, who have enriched my life;

to their parents, who have pushed me to keep on looking for answers to their many questions and problems;

to other like-minded people who are striving to provide a better quality of life for children with disabilities;

and to my family and friends, who have never stopped believing in me.

~ CONTENTS ~

About the Author iii

Introduction v

1. General Coping Strategies 1

Relax 1
Don't blame yourself 2
Don't dwell on the negative 4
Don't be over protective or possessive 5
Make time for yourselves 7
Find out as much as possible about your child's problem 9
Don't be ashamed of, or embarrassed by, your child 10
Don't be afraid to ask for help 12
Don't look too far ahead 13
Look after yourselves 15
Trust your own instincts 17
Try to see your child first and foremost as a child 19

2. The Need for Stimulation and Interaction 21

3. Encouraging Physical Development 25

Part 1: Preventative Measures 26
Put your child down 26
Change positions regularly 27
Keep things moving 32
Choose equipment carefully 34

Part 2: Encourage Independent Movement 36
The development of mobility 36
Give your child opportunity to move 37
Make it easy for your child to move 38
Give your child a reason to move 41
Give assistance where necessary 43
Stimulate your child's balance 46

4. Encouraging intellectual development 49

Part 1: Input of Information 51
Stimulate the senses 51
Vision 52
Hearing 53
Touch 53
Taste and smell 54
Combining the senses 55

Provide contrasts *55*
Vary the direction of stimulus *56*
Talk to your child *57*
Introduce your child to books *59*

Part 2: Opportunities for Output **61**
Help your child to explore his environment *61*
Anticipate his questions *62*
Learn to recognise his responses *64*
Include him in conversation *66*
Let him show you what he knows *67*
Give your child choices *69*

5. Encouraging Social Development **71**
Don't underestimate your child *72*
Discourage your child from becoming "clingy" *73*
Encourage interaction with your child *75*
Introduce your child to different social situations ... *76*
Help your child become aware of himself *77*
Encourage give-and-take *78*
Teach your child to respect others *80*
Don't lose sight of what is "normal" *81*

6. Encouraging Self-Help **83**
Don't keep your child a baby *83*
Establish proper sleeping and waking times *84*
Push the pace with feeding *86*
The question of toilet training *89*
Motivation and a sense of achievement *91*
Recognise and avoid "learned helplessness" *92*
Independence – the ultimate goal *93*

7. Encouraging Good Behaviour **95**
Understanding the need *96*
What is good behaviour? *97*
Moulding behaviour *98*
Consistency is the key *99*
Giving the right attention *100*
Choose rewards carefully *103*
The same rules for all the family *104*

In summary *105*

A Final Message *107*

Useful Contacts *108*

ABOUT THE AUTHOR

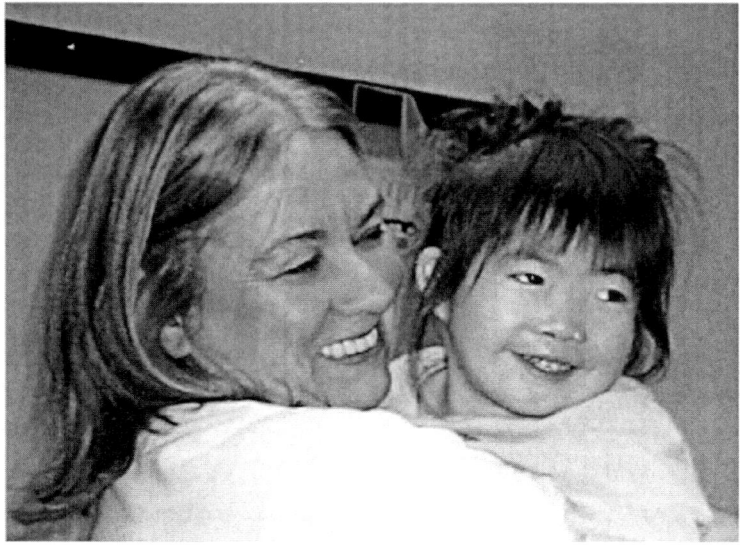

Margaret Barrett originally qualified as a teacher of mentally handicapped children in Manchester and went on to teach children with multiple handicaps. She then underwent two years training in developmental education in the USA and on her return to the UK worked for a number of charities concerned with brain injured children.

During her career she has helped children in several countries including Switzerland, Australia, Italy, Finland and Japan.

Today Margaret is based in South Wales where she runs her consultancy **Developmental Intervention**, and she still makes regular visits to Japan to work with families there. She is also in close contact with the founders of the Willem Group at the Australian Institute for the Achievement of Human Potential in Victoria.

INTRODUCTION

The very fact that you are taking the time to look at this book suggests that you, or somebody close to you, has been touched by the possibility of something being wrong with their child. If that is the case, you are probably at the beginning of a long quest to find out what you can do and where you can go for help.

Whether this is your first or fifth baby, whether you are a novice parent or an experienced grandparent, the path is likely to be equally long and hazardous.

This book has been written primarily for parents who have been told that their child is suffering, or likely to suffer, some form of disability, but it could also be useful for other relatives and friends of the family, as well as being of interest to those in the caring professions.

The cause of the disability might be brain damage, a genetic or chromosomal disorder, metabolic disease or traumatic injury. The symptoms shown can include such things as cerebral palsy, developmental delay, sensory impairment, movement disorder and learning difficulty.

Whatever the cause and symptoms, one thing all of you who find yourselves in this situation will have in common is the feeling of devastation, helplessness and uncertainty.

Some of you will have known from very soon after the birth – or even, in some cases, in the latter stages of pregnancy – that there are problems. Whilst for some parents this will be seen as beneficial – in that they can quickly get to grips with the situation and be directed towards agencies offering help – for others the shock is overwhelming and can delay or even halt the bonding process, as they try to come to terms with the fact that this is not going to be the normal healthy baby they were expecting.

Generally speaking, though, finding out quickly means that you might immediately have lowered your expectations in respect of your child's development and adopted the "any progress, however slight, will be welcome" attitude.

Some of you will have endured – and indeed may still be enduring – months of feeling instinctively that things are not right before obtaining confirmation of your suspicions from a medical professional. It might be argued that this scenario is easier to cope with, in that you will already have bonded with the baby before having to face up to the difficulties ahead, but this can be counterbalanced by an increasing lack of confidence and feelings of inadequacy if people fail to take your concerns seriously.

While you will most probably have started out with normal expectations for your child, your introduction to disability will have been via his continued failure to reach milestones, which might result in a "he will never be able to achieve anything" frame of mind.

Then there are those of you who, in an instant – a squeal of brakes, a sudden illness, a bang on the head – will have had to come to terms with the loss of the energetic, outgoing child you knew and in his place accept one who is as helpless and dependent as a newborn. As well as having to learn how physically to care for your child, you will have had to replace the prospect of university and a career with the hope that he might regain some mobility and learn to communicate again.

In some cases there might be the additional agony of overwhelming feelings of guilt – you should have held onto him to prevent him running into the road, you should have noticed his high fever sooner, you should have stopped him from climbing … etc.

Only too often, parents and close family members become so bogged down by disability, so wrapped up in hospital appointments, so bound by times of administering medication, so afraid that they will not be able to cope or cater for the child's needs, that they end up seeing the child as a problem and failing to recognise what is, very often, a dear little personality within.

To me, this is nothing less than a tragedy, since childhood is precious whatever the situation, and something that can never be relived or recaptured.

If I have one hope for this book, it is that it will help at least a few parents to find ways of coping with the prospect of raising a child with disabilities and enable them to still experience the pleasures and pride that should be theirs by right.

The following pages contain some points which you should try to bear in mind as you are caring for your disabled baby. They are not listed in any order of priority, as you will find that different aspects assume greater degrees of importance for you personally at various stages of your child's development.

Some of the points covered, you will see as common sense – general procedures you would automatically have carried out anyway – others, you might find, are new concepts seen from a more objective viewpoint than your own.

None of them are intended to be a magic formula to suddenly remove the problems associated with being the parents of a baby with a disability, but it is hoped that at least some of them may help you put things into perspective and make it a little easier for you to cope with the situation on a day to day basis.

I apologise for the fact that, throughout this book, I have referred to the child as "he" – this in no way detracts from the value and importance of little girls, it simply makes the manuscript easier to read. I have also frequently used the term "baby" although, in reality, the same principles apply to parents of all newly diagnosed children, whatever their age, and even to those who were half way through successfully rearing an able-bodied child before tragedy struck. You might also find that I have, on some occasions, repeated myself, since some of the points raised fall into different categories and have therefore been dealt with in more than one chapter.

Whether you read this book from cover to cover, dip into chapters as you feel them to be relevant, or come back to the contents time and time again for reassurance, I hope that somewhere within these pages you will find some useful guidance and support which will enable you to become the relaxed and confident parent your disabled child is going to need.

Margaret Barrett
South Wales, November 2008

1. General Coping Strategies

When you first learn that you are the parent of a baby with disabilities, your immediate reaction will, most probably, be that you won't be able to cope, either with the whole concept or with the day-to-day practicalities.

This is entirely understandable but in most cases quite unfounded. You will find that you can, in fact, take many things in your stride, almost without realising it.

The aim of this chapter is to give you some pointers that might help to reduce your anxiety and establish routines which could make the coping process easier for all concerned.

Relax

However young or severely disabled your child may be, you can be sure that he will very quickly pick up tensions, moods and anxieties from those around him. If you lack confidence when handling your baby, he will feel insecure – and an insecure baby cries!

Your baby may feel stiffer or floppier than others you have handled, which can be disconcerting, and you are bound to feel awkward at first, but it is simply a matter of both of you learning to feel at ease with one another.

Try to set time aside to make sure you are in a comfortable position and simply hold your child – if necessary, surrounding you both with pillows or cushions to take the weight – so that you can feel your arms and body relax. As you feel the tension leave your limbs, so you should begin to feel a corresponding relaxation in your child and he should gradually become more settled.

Experiment also with walking around the house, holding your baby in different positions until you find one or two that you are both happy with. He won't break, and since you are, in effect, going to be working together as a partnership, it is important that you start to communicate with each other, albeit at a pretty basic level, at an early stage.

In the same way, you also need to learn to relax emotionally with your child. If his constant crying is really getting to you and making you uptight, no amount of holding him, walking the floor with him or generally trying to pacify him will have any lasting effect. Instead, try to recognise when you have reached stalemate; put him down for a while, in a safe place but out of immediate earshot, and sit down with a cup of coffee and a magazine.

The time to return to him is when you have felt yourself calm down enough to be able to smile and talk soothingly, which will have more chance of providing the reassurance he is seeking.

Don't be afraid to let a baby cry just because he is disabled.

Don't blame yourself

For many parents of a child with disabilities there is a grave tendency to blame themselves for just about everything, starting with the cause of his problems in the first place. Many parents agonise over what they may have done or not done prior to or during the pregnancy; what measures they should have insisted on during the birth; what problems they should have noticed during early development; or, in the case of children suffering traumatic injury, what safety precautions they could or should have taken to safeguard against accidents.

In the vast majority of cases, no blame whatsoever can or should be apportioned to the parents and even in those rare cases where their actions may have unwittingly contributed to their child's problems, to dwell on this and continually hold themselves responsible is totally counterproductive.

In order to effectively help your child, you need to be only concerned with the present and the future. Becoming absorbed in the whys and wherefores of what has already happened can only serve to hold all of you back. Also, if you continue to hold yourself responsible for your child's disability you will eventually become so consumed by guilt that you will cease to be objective about the child himself and will spend your life trying to make amends for what you believe you have inflicted on him.

In a similar way, parents often assume responsibility for every additional problem their child suffers – if he is miserable, it is because they failed to make him happy; if he is ill, it is because they failed to take adequate care of him; if he falls over, it is because they were not watchful enough.

If any or all of these things were to happen to an able-bodied child you would, in all probability, simply accept them as things to be expected when you have children. Why should it be any different in the case of a disabled child?

You need to accept and come to terms with the fact that having a disability does not automatically make your child immune to all other problems associated with childhood, and that when these problems occur they are not your fault. Taking the blame for everything will result in an inability to enjoy any aspect of your child and his development, which would be a great shame.

Don't dwell on the negative

From the moment your child is diagnosed as having a disability you will find that the world is full of people who are intent on reminding you about what he can't do and what he is unlikely to be able to do in the future. This can take the form of innocent questions from other parents, such as "can't he sit yet?" or "doesn't he say anything?" – or bolder statements from professionals, such as "of course, you must realise that he has very little understanding" or, even more depressingly, "it is unlikely that he will *ever* walk" or "don't expect him to be able to lead an independent life".

It is hardly surprising that in this environment parents find it difficult to view their child in a positive light, but this is something you should really make a conscious effort to do.

Try to focus on all the things he *can* do, however small or insignificant they may appear to be, and use these abilities as a starting point to encourage further development. When people point out something that your child is *not* able to do, quickly respond with something he *has* achieved.

For instance, when asked if he can sit, you might reply, "No, but he has learned to hold his head up". Similarly, the observation that he doesn't say anything could be met with "even though he doesn't speak, he does understand what I say to him".

If you consistently change the tone of the conversation to be more positive, you will find that, in time, other people's attitudes towards your child will also change.

Along the same lines, don't fall into the trap yourself of underestimating your child just because you have been told that he doesn't understand. Sometimes parents start to feel that their child is, in fact, understanding what they say to him, but then convince themselves that this is nothing more than wishful thinking on their part because doctors have pointed out the degree of intellectual impairment he is likely to suffer.

Other parents have admitted that they were afraid to say that they felt their child, who had severe physical difficulties, might in fact be quite intelligent, in case other people thought they were foolish or unrealistic.

Be positive. If you have a glimmer of a feeling that your child is responding to you, then believe that he is and give him more stimulation to encourage further response.

One thing to be sure of is that if you, his parents, don't believe in him, then nobody else will.

Sadly, there are many instances where parents are told that the severity of their child's disability is so great that there is really nothing they can do for him other than to take him home and love him, and to expect little by way of progress.

The tragedy is that from this moment on, if this advice is taken seriously, he is effectively denied the chance of proving this prognosis to be wrong, since a child who is constantly held, cuddled and cosseted by parents who have little or no expectations of him will have very little opportunity for development of any kind.

Don't be over protective or possessive

When you know that your child is disabled, your instinct as a parent is to protect him from anything and anybody that may cause him additional pain, discomfort or unhappiness. However, it is very easy to carry this to extremes, and in so doing to compound the problems for both your child and yourselves.

There is a very fine line to be drawn between taking sensible steps to safeguard and shield your child and 'wrapping him in cotton wool' to the extent that you actually deprive him of experiences that are an essential part of his development.

No baby ever learned to sit, crawl or walk without taking the occasional tumble. Very few young children manage to get through more than a day or so without shedding tears. Yet despite this, the vast majority grow up to be happy, well balanced individuals who show no lasting ill effects from life's little set-backs.

By protecting your disabled child to the extent that nothing unpleasant is ever allowed to happen to him, you are giving him a very false impression of the world in which he is eventually going to have to find his place, and when, sooner or later, he has to face disappointment, pain or rejection, he will find it much harder to bear or to understand.

In terms of being too possessive with your child, it is very understandable for you to feel that nobody can handle him, comfort him, anticipate his needs and generally care for him in quite the same way as you, his parents. Whilst this is, in all probability, quite true, it is really not in the interest of either your child or yourselves to restrict his exposure to other people.

From the child's point of view, it is important that he understands and accepts that he has to do things for other people as well as for you. Suppose for a moment that you are the only one who can feed him, the only one who can settle him to sleep, the only one who can stop him crying. Now suppose that you are suddenly taken ill, or that some emergency makes it imperative for you to be away from him for a while. How will he survive? How long can he go without eating before doctors are forced to resort to feeding by tube? Will he cry himself to sleep each night? Will he get himself into such a state that he makes himself ill?

Now ask yourself which, in the long term, is going to cause him (and ultimately yourselves) the most unhappiness – getting him used to being handled by different people in different ways, even though neither he nor you may always like or want it, or suddenly having his secure, comfortable little world turned upside down, possibly with long lasting repercussions?

You should also consider the possibility that by doing everything for your child all of the time you face the danger of ceasing to be objective about him and anticipating his wants to such an extent that he no longer needs to try to communicate them. It would be a shame to thwart his development in this way.

Make time for yourselves

In some ways this is an extension of the previous point, in that it relates to the danger of being too possessive, but this time looking at it more from your own point of view than your child's.

For the majority of parents reading this book, the commitment to care for your child will be a long-term one, and in order for you to be able to carry this through successfully it is essential that you do not allow him to take over every aspect of your lives.

There are several reasons for this.

Firstly, to keep things in perspective and prevent yourselves from becoming totally bogged down by the whole situation, it will be vital that you can retain a sense of humour, and the only way you can do this is to have interests and a part of your life that do not revolve around your child and his problems.

Secondly, you are going to need the long term support of family and friends, and this can be difficult to maintain if your only topic of conversation and interest is your child.

Thirdly, although you might like to think otherwise, you are, at the end of the day, only human and there are limits to what you can realistically cope with.

Taking regular breaks from your child, however short they may be, will effectively recharge your batteries and enable you to keep going for a longer period of time.

Fourthly, you must always remember that your disabled child is only one member of your family and that partners, other children and parents, etc, also need your attention and time. Failing to recognise this will, in time, blow the whole family apart and cause immense resentment of the child who is seen to be the cause of the problem.

Finally, and by no means least in importance – in order to properly stimulate and encourage your child's development, you yourselves need to be lively and interesting, and this is very difficult if all your time is spent caring for him and discussing his problems.

Bearing these points in mind, you should put aside any feelings of guilt at leaving him and take up all offers from family and trusted friends to babysit, take him out or have him to stay overnight. Not only will this give you time for yourselves, it will allow others to become more involved with your child and feel that they are contributing to the quality of his life.

At the same time it will get him used to the idea that your lives do not totally revolve around him.

Don't turn down offers of help on the grounds that you have nowhere to go. Spending time alone at home, reading or watching a film, without interruption, enjoying a leisurely meal together or simply catching up on much-needed rest can often be a refreshing break.

Find out as much as possible about your child's problem

If you are to be able to effectively help your child and, at the same time, come to terms with what has happened to him, it is important that you have as much information as possible about his condition and the nature of his problems.

How easy you will find it to obtain this information will depend on a number of variables, including how well you communicate with your doctors, how well informed they are on the subject, how much you are prepared to read and research yourselves and whether or not you come into contact with other families with a child with similar problems.

One thing that appears to be common to most families is that information of this kind is not automatically offered to them, it is generally only given in response to their questions. This means, of course, that those who are naturally shy or who find themselves somewhat in awe of professionals are the ones who finish up with the least information.

We have all experienced situations where we have gone into a consultation determined to ask a million and one questions only to realise afterwards that the most vital ones have been forgotten in the general anxiety of the discussion.

Prior to any visit to a doctor, therapist, teacher or other professional dealing with your child, it is a good idea to sit down and prepare a list of all the points you want to raise and questions you want to ask.

If the answers you are given do not satisfy you or confuse you, *keep on asking* until you are happy with the explanation given.

If you feel that the person you are talking to does not know the answer to your question *ask to be referred* to somebody who can supply the necessary information.

If you are being advised in respect of a particular form of treatment, surgical procedure or schooling option and are uncertain or confused about what you should do, *ask for a second opinion* – unless the situation is life-threatening it is far better to delay action until you are happy with what is happening than to have to live with the consequences of a decision made in haste and based on inadequate information.

You should remember that the professionals you go to for advice are also only human and do not always have all the answers.

Don't be ashamed of, or embarrassed by, your child

There is probably not a parent on earth who has not been both ashamed of or embarrassed by their able-bodied offspring on numerous occasions – and there will no doubt be times when this applies in respect of your disabled child.

The important thing to determine is whether your emotions are brought about by your child's actions or behaviour on a particular occasion, which is perfectly valid and acceptable, or whether they relate more to the fact that that he has a disability. This is a question you need to try and answer honestly, because if you allow your child's condition to become a constant source of embarrassment to you, then you will find that it gradually starts to invade and affect all aspects of your lives.

You must try and establish exactly what is the cause of your embarrassment. Do you feel that having a disabled child in some way suggests that you are inadequate as parents? Do you feel that people are looking at you and pitying you? Or is it simply that having a child who is obviously different attracts unwelcome attention to you?

Whatever the source, it is important that you take steps to overcome these emotions so that you can enjoy life with your child rather than constantly feeling the need to hide him away or continually apologise for him.

First and foremost, having a disabled child is, in itself, nothing at all to be ashamed of. It can happen to any person, from any background and walk of life, at any time. We have already discussed the futility of trying to apportion blame and how persisting along this line only promotes feelings of failure and shame. Your child may be suffering disabilities, but this should not in any way detract from his significance and value as a person in his own right, and to be ashamed of him in some way suggests that you consider him to be inferior or substandard.

Be proud of him, purely for being your child, irrespective of his difficulties, abilities or appearance. One of the greatest things you can do for him is to help him develop self-respect and a feeling of self-worth, and this will only happen if he grows up secure in the knowledge that, as well as loving him, you respect and value him as a member of your family and take pride in his achievements, however limited they might be.

One of the major sources of embarrassment for parents of disabled children is to come face to face with people who are themselves embarrassed by the situation. However, there is a very important factor to be aware of here. In the vast majority of cases the embarrassment they are showing has very little to do with the child and his problems, it is more a reflection of the fact that they themselves do not know how to react.

People often become extremely self-conscious when talking to someone who is unable to respond or communicate in "normal" ways and the best approach is to confront the problem head on by taking the lead and demonstrating that neither you nor your child is embarrassed by the situation, so there is no need for the onlooker to be either.

You will be surprised how quickly embarrassment can turn to admiration and respect when people are made to feel more comfortable.

If disabled children are ever going to be fully accepted by and integrated into society their parents are going to have to play a large part in educating the public and helping them to understand and come to terms with disability.

Don't be afraid to ask for help

Many parents feel that their disabled child is their responsibility and theirs alone and that asking for assistance of any kind amounts to an admission that they are unable to cope.

If you share this view, you should very quickly put it out of your mind, since it is a fact of life that everybody needs help at some stage and you should feel free to ask for it without feeling that you have, in some way, failed.

There may be a wide variety of help available from statutory bodies and/or voluntary organisations but it is important to remember that, by requesting assistance, you will not be seen as inadequate parents.

The help can take various forms – it may be the provision of specialist equipment or financial assistance towards transport – or it may be of a more practical nature, such as respite care to allow a break for you and/or the rest of the family. Some help may be of a professional nature but it can also be provided by family or friends.

The important thing is for you to recognise when you need assistance rather than trying to struggle on alone until you reach breaking point. Think of the old proverb "a stitch in time saves nine". Minor assistance at an early stage could prevent a major rescue operation later on.

Don't look too far ahead

Once you know that your child has a disability you will be very aware of the responsibility that this entails for you and that this will continue, in all probability, for the rest of your lives.

Whilst it is obviously essential that you do, from time to time, discuss the long-term future and ensure that adequate provision is made for your child, together with clear instructions in respect of your wishes for his continuing care in the event of anything happening to yourselves, it is important that you do not become so depressed by the thought of the long, hard road ahead of you all that you are unable to think positively about his immediate future.

It should also be said that in some cases children make amazing progress, despite what the parents have been told to expect, and in those instances they could have been spared the heartache of hours spent considering a dismal outcome for their child.

Another problem with worrying too much about the future is that you run the risk of talking yourselves into believing that you will not be able to cope as your child grows older and bigger.

Handling a small baby or young child is one thing but lifting and carrying a large immobile teenager is an entirely different prospect!

There are two points to remember here.

The first is, never assume that your child is not going to learn to get around by himself and at least be able to contribute to his daily care and lifestyle. If you do, you are already falling into the trap of being negative about him, which we discussed earlier.

Also, none of us can predict what advances may be made in coming years in respect of treatment, therapy, aids and appliances that may help to alleviate many of the current problems associated with disability.

The second point is that even if progress does not occur and your child does not become independently mobile, you are not just suddenly one day going to be presented with a child too large to cope with. His growth is going to be a very gradual process which you will adapt to over a long period of time and you will find that little changes to your lifting and handling techniques occur naturally as you go along, so that the increase in size and weight is almost imperceptible.

When you are first told that your child has a severe problem your mind automatically focuses on the downside, such as what sacrifices you will have to make and how much of yourselves you will have to give with the possibility of little return.

At this stage you cannot appreciate or even understand the fact that you will probably gain an awful lot from your child in ways that are as yet inconceivable. Many parents come to realise over the years that, far from being a burden, their child with disabilities has, in fact, not only enjoyed a fulfilling and happy life but has also enriched the lives of other members of the family beyond measure.

We all have dreams and aspirations for our children, but in reality we don't know what is waiting round the corner for any of them, with or without disabilities.

Looking too far into the future can result in a lot of valuable time being wasted worrying about problems which may, in fact, never occur and – even more importantly – can rob you of precious hours spent getting to know and enjoy your child.

Look after yourselves

As was pointed out at the start of the previous section, you are, as parents, already very much aware of the long-term responsibility of caring for a disabled child. However, in order to provide for him to the best of your ability you also have a responsibility to yourselves, and the importance of looking after yourselves cannot be stressed enough. What use will you be to your child if you put yourselves under such continual strain that your own health fails? How can you take care of him if you find yourself in the situation that you need to be taken care of yourself? How will you get him in and out of his chair if you have consistently used such bad lifting techniques that your back is permanently damaged?

This applies just as much to mental and emotional stress as it does to physical strain. How can you teach him to feel positive about himself if you are so depressed that you can only see the negative side of him? How will you encourage him to take note of what is going on in the world around him if you yourself have lost interest in everything outside your own immediate problems?

Having a disabled child does not miraculously transform you into super-humans. Nobody expects you to be able to carry on indefinitely and you should not expect it of yourselves.

It is vital that you learn to recognise when you need to rest, ask for help, seek medical advice in respect of your own health or simply switch off. It is also important that you eat sensibly to build up your own resistance to infection.

Another essential requirement is sleep. The fastest way to wear somebody down is to deprive them of sleep for a prolonged period of time. We can all cope with most things during the day if we are reasonably refreshed from a restful night, and can even adjust over time to a long-term reduction in our sleep requirements, but if our sleep is consistently and continually disturbed then even the smallest irritation that we would normally have taken in our stride becomes a problem of mammoth proportions.

If you have had so many broken nights that you find you are permanently tired and irritable and are snapping at all members of the family, including your disabled child, you have probably reached the stage where you need the intervention of somebody else taking charge of him for a couple of nights, whether it be someone from within your circle of family and friends or respite care.

This should not be seen as an admission of defeat but more as a sensible safety precaution. If that turns out to be impossible to organise, the very least you should do is arrange for someone to look after him for a few hours during the day and make yourself go and lie down. You will probably feel that you are being idle and be tempted to use the time to catch up on chores you have not been able to complete, but this will defeat the whole object. The time will be far more usefully spent catching up on sleep – and believe me, given the right environment and opportunity you will have no difficulty drifting off!

Trust your own instincts

Many parents who instinctively know how to handle and cope with their fit and healthy children suddenly find themselves floundering and uncertain about what they should do with the one who is disabled. This is often related not so much to the child's disabilities as to their own feelings of inadequacy and inexperience and a fear of doing the wrong thing, and in some way making his problems worse.

You must learn to believe in yourselves and trust your instincts as parents to know what is best for this child in just the same way as with your other children – although this will of course be much more difficult if it is your first child who is disabled or if you generally lack confidence in your abilities as a parent.

Sadly, in many instances, the need to rely on your own intuition and follow your instincts becomes apparent very early on in your disabled child's life (or in some cases immediately, if the disability is the result of an illness or accident). For the vast majority of families, the initial suspicion that all is 'not quite right' with their child comes from a parent or grandparent, but they then face an uphill struggle to convince others, especially professionals, that their fears may in fact be justified. Only too often they are told that they are over anxious or expecting too much, and to bring the child back in six months if they are still concerned.

For many parents, this is the start of a lack of confidence in their own judgement, and several have reported to me that after months of repeatedly trying to get somebody to believe that there is something wrong with their child they have started to question whether, in fact, they are the ones who have a problem. When eventually they were told that the their child was, indeed, disabled – and in some cases quite severely, despite a previous reluctance on the part of the professionals to accept that there was any problem at all – the shock and pain was somewhat tinged with relief that they had actually been right all along – quickly followed by anger and frustration that so much precious time had been wasted.

The need to trust your own judgement also applies very much to the day-to-day handling of your child. If your usual way of dealing with a baby who persistently cries – although you are quite sure that he is not hungry, wet, sick or uncomfortable – is to leave him to cry for a while, then that is the approach you should adopt with your disabled baby too.

If a temper tantrum or bad behaviour would normally evoke a stern rebuke from you, then your child's disabilities should not automatically protect him from this. It is important for him and his brothers and sisters to realise that while his disabilities might, in many ways, single him out for special attention, they do not entitle him to preferential treatment when it comes to behaviour and discipline.

As parents of a disabled child you will be given no end of advice from a whole variety of sources, both professional and otherwise. Whilst most, if not all of it, will be given with the best of intentions, a good deal of it will be unrequested, unnecessary, misleading, confusing and in some cases downright contradictory.

You must always remember that, at the end of the day, he is your child and your responsibility and that you are under no obligation to take or act upon any advice that you are given if your instincts are telling you that it is not in your child's best interests or right for you as a family.

Try to see your child first and foremost as a child

This is possibly the most important point in this book and probably the most difficult to put into words.

There is no question that having a child with disabilities places additional strain on the whole family and makes the parents far more aware of their responsibilities. However, do try hard not to always look at him from the point of view of being disabled but try to see him for what he is – a child like any other, who just happens to have some difficulties.

If you are unable to see him in this light, you will miss out on a lot of the joy and pleasure that any child can bring to his parents, and a disabled child is, in his own way, just as capable of doing that as any other.

If you keep your child's disability to the forefront of your mind all the time, there is a very real danger that you will forget that he is, after all, only a child, and not realise that a lot of the things he is doing are a product of childhood rather than of disability.

Don't make him old before his time; he will have to come to terms with the realities of his life soon enough and childhood should be a time of laughter and innocence – something none of us can ever recapture later in life.

The life of any child should be seen as precious and none the less so because he happens to be disabled. It is up to all of us to ensure that the quality of that life is as rich and full as it can possibly be, and that can only be achieved if he is loved and appreciated for the person that he is and not seen merely as a collection of disabilities.

Your disabled child need not be an encumbrance – he can actually enhance your lives … if you will allow him to!

2. The Need for Stimulation and Interaction

The purpose of this small chapter is to set the scene for the ones that follow but if you fail to realise its significance the remainder of the book will be of little or no consequence.

Stimulation and interaction are essential requirements for the development of all human beings, either with or without disabilities. It is a well-known and accepted fact that babies and young children deprived of stimulation do not develop as quickly or as fully as those exposed to a variety of visual, auditory and tactile stimuli.

If this is true of a baby born with all his senses and faculties intact, imagine the impact on one who is already struggling to make sense of his environment because of a restricted ability to see, hear, feel or move.

Over the years there have been a number of recorded instances of children discovered locked away in isolation who, when discovered and subsequently rescued, appear unable to comprehend or communicate and even, on some occasions, to walk. There is nothing inherently wrong with these children but the circumstances in which they have been existing have offered little or no opportunity for learning.

If we were to take any newly born baby and immediately place him alone in a cot in a dark room, handling him only for feeding, changing and dressing, all of which we carried out in silence, and to then bring him out on his first birthday, what stage of development do you think he would have reached? Would he, like most other 12-month-olds, be sitting up and crawling around, maybe pulling himself to his feet and walking around the furniture? Would his eyes shine with curiosity as he looked at his surroundings and made eye contact with people? Would he respond to his name and being spoken to by laughing and babbling? Would he be constantly picking things up and examining them, taking everything to his mouth before discarding and moving on to something else? Would he freely demonstrate his emotions, giggling with delight one minute and screaming in anger the next? Would he be shy with strangers and clearly show his likes and dislikes, not only in respect of people but also food, toys and activities?

Even if you have no experience whatsoever of how babies develop and have never considered for a moment the questions posed in the previous paragraph, I think that if you were to really think about it you would instinctively come up with the answers.

Babies develop muscle tone, head control and the ability to move by being handled and put into different positions. They learn to look at things with interest if there are lots of different things to look at and to recognise and respond to sounds when they are hearing different noises, voices, tones and words. They are encouraged to make different sounds by the responses their vocalisations produce from others and they learn about objects around them by touching, holding, tasting and smelling. They begin to express emotions when they realise that doing so can have an effect on what happens next – giggling happily might result in a pleasurable activity being repeated while screams could effectively bring an end to something he doesn't like.

Our baby who has been kept in silent, dark isolation is unlikely to have developed to anywhere near this level. The chances are he will be floppy with poor head control and unable to sit, since he will have spent all his time lying down. He won't be crawling because the restricted space in his cot will not have allowed for this. His eyes will be dull, he will show little interest in anything or anybody around him, he will be slow to turn to sounds and he will look blankly if you speak to him. He will, most probably, be very quiet and will make little or no attempt to reach out to anything you might try to entice him with. He will appear expressionless, it will be difficult, if not impossible, to make him smile and he will seem without emotion to the point of not even crying, because any tears he has shed will have gone unheeded.

After just a year without stimulation, this normal, healthy baby is way behind his peers and is already functioning as though he has considerable disabilities.

No parent reading this book would consciously or willingly subject their child to such a harsh, uncompromising, unstimulating environment, but I would like you to think for a moment about how his disabilities themselves might, in effect, be doing just that.

If he has restricted or limited vision, he is probably not able to focus on faces or objects or to concentrate on one particular thing within his visual range.

If he cannot turn his head, he won't be able to choose another view to look at, so the visual stimulation available to him is very limited.

If he can't hear very well, is unable to attend to particular sounds or cannot differentiate between variations in tone or volume, he will be lacking in meaningful auditory stimulation.

If he can't move his limbs, use his hands or move around the floor, his sense of touch will be diminished, which means he will be receiving limited or distorted tactile stimulation.

All of this can result in him being denied appropriate input of information, which in turn might result in a lack of interest in his surroundings and an inability to interact or effectively respond.

It is hoped that once the need for stimulation and interaction is understood, the following chapters will make it easier for parents and other members of the family to find and expand ways of encouraging their child's development, while at the same time building more natural and meaningful relationships with him.

3. Encouraging Physical Development

When a child is diagnosed as suffering from a brain injury, it is often some considerable time before it can be ascertained whether or not he is going to be affected physically and, if so, to what degree. It is only with the passage of time that a failure to develop mobility or a stiffening of limbs becomes apparent and, sadly, by then a lot of valuable time may have been lost.

This is equally true in cases of traumatic injury, where the patient may remain in a semi-comatose state for days, weeks or even months before the full extent of the permanent damage suffered can be assessed. In both instances, proper handling and positioning from the beginning could lessen, or even avoid, problems occurring later in life and provide opportunities for the development of movement. However, until it becomes evident that intervention from professionals such as physiotherapists, etc, is going to be necessary, parents and family are at a loss to know what to do that might help.

This section has been divided into two parts. The first deals with simple measures that can be taken to help maintain the body in good condition, stimulate the development of muscle tone and prevent the onset of contractures and other deformities. The second attempts to give ideas on how to encourage the development of independent movement and mobility and how to motivate the child to want to do more for himself.

The advice given here should in no way replace any therapeutic treatment being offered, it is simply showing ways in which families can contribute to their child's physical wellbeing from a very early stage.

Part 1: Preventative Measures

Put your child down

For many families, being told that their child is disabled leads to them quickly falling into the trap of feeling that for some reason it is wrong to put him down, that he should be held as much as possible or at least be propped into the corner of a chair or sofa surrounded by cushions.

This is wrong for the child for a variety of reasons.

By continually holding your child you are inhibiting the movement of his limbs and preventing him from stretching out his body. If he does not have the ability to support himself, his spine will be pushed into unnatural alignments as you shift him around to find positions more comfortable for both of you. Any attempts he might make at kicking his legs or waving his arms will probably result in you changing his position, which means that he is unable to learn from his movements. Opportunities for him to develop head control will be limited, since being held will usually mean that his head is supported, or that if it flops you will quickly adjust his position to compensate. Holding a child also usually results in his body being, to some extent, compressed, so that he finds it more difficult to take deep breaths and to control dribbling.

By putting your child down for periods of time on a flat surface, you are allowing him the opportunity to learn about his own body, to experiment with movements of his limbs and to experience the feeling of freedom to move as opposed to restriction. Lying flat also allows for proper alignment of the spine and makes it easier for him to turn his head from side to side, while at the same time enabling full expansion of his lungs if he needs to take a deep breath.

Obviously, your child is not necessarily going to readily accept being put down, especially if by the time you start to put this into practice he has become used to being held, so don't be surprised if the first few attempts are met with howls of protest. However, no child is in a position to understand or judge what is in his long term interests, so it is important that you persevere. Don't feel that you are being cruel or abandoning him by putting him down, and indeed you can give him just as much attention when he is on the floor as when you are holding him, by getting down with him and touching, talking, playing and giving him things to look at. If you tackle it in a positive way, he will soon come to accept being put down.

Change positions regularly

Having stressed the importance of putting your child down, there will, of course, be many occasions when you do hold him, either by choice or from necessity. It is, however, most important that you do not repeatedly hold him in the same position, even if avoiding this results in some minor discomfort for either or both of you.

Again, there are a variety of reasons for this.

If, when you have your child on your lap, you always hold him facing the same way, supported by the same arm, as he grows his spine will eventually begin to curve as he moulds to the shape and position of your body. Also, if he wants to try and reach out to touch your face, or indeed to do anything with his hands, he may be restricted to only being able to develop the use of one side, as the other is arm is always caught between the two of you – and incidentally, the hand he is, in effect, being forced to use may not be his most functional one!

Another potential problem is that, because he must always turn his head in the same direction in order to look around, he may develop a tendency to permanently hold it to one side, which could eventually result in an inability to turn the other way.

One extreme illustration of what continually holding a child in the same position can lead to is worth reporting here. Some years ago a two-year-old boy suffered severe brain damage following an illness and, after his condition had stabilised, he was returned to his parents to care for him at home. Although he was left unable to move, he did not, at that time, show signs of stiffness or spasticity, and his family were given no specific instructions as to how to care for him, but warned not to expect too much progress. His parents were naturally devastated by what had happened to their little boy and found it very difficult to adjust to suddenly being responsible for a disabled child.

They were at a loss as to how they could help him and so did the one thing that came naturally to them – they showered him with love. From the day he returned home from hospital he was never left alone, being passed backwards and forwards between various members of his family who spent hours talking to him and playing with him. Unfortunately, whilst this was undoubtedly the right thing to do to encourage him to respond to them, they made a basic error in that each person held him in exactly the same way and the same position because "that was how he liked to be held".

The result was that, by the time the child was seven years old, his body had taken on the shape of a 'C' curve. Because he had always been supported by the adult's left arm and leaned towards them to his right, pushing his spine out to the left, his right shoulder had become dislocated from being wedged by the adult's body and his head twisted to the left in an attempt to see what was going on. One hip was also dislocated, his legs were tightly scissored and any attempt to stretch or straighten him produced great distress. Since his growth had been gradual over the years, nobody had noticed that his increase in length meant that his body must curve in order for him to adopt the same position.

Thus, tragically, this well-meaning family had, albeit in total ignorance, contributed in a significant way to their son's compounded problems. Had they been aware of this from the start, whilst he may still have been immobile he would undoubtedly have been more comfortable and easier to handle, as well as being in a better position to benefit from future treatment or therapeutic measures.

This case is an extreme illustration and it is unlikely that today a family would find themselves so completely without advice in respect of handling their disabled child. However, it is worth bearing in mind when considering how to hold your child.

It is equally important to think about position when putting your child down to rest or play. If you always lay him on his left side, you are only allowing him the use of his right arm and leg; if each time you prop him on the sofa you wedge him into the same corner, you will encourage him to always lean to the same side; if when you lay him face down you always turn his head to face the same direction, you will find that it becomes increasingly difficult to turn it the other way.

You should also bear in mind that if your child has little or no voluntary movement he may become very uncomfortable if left in the same position for too long. Just think how you feel if you have been slouched in a chair for half an hour or so and imagine what it might be like if you could not shift around, stretch or change your position.

A further relevant point is that your child may find it easier to carry out various movements or tasks in certain positions, so when putting him down you should think about what he will be trying to do.

Changing position also applies to how you carry your child around. If, for instance, you always hold him in your right arm, in the upright position so that he rests against your right shoulder, you will encourage him not only to always curve to the same side but also to keep his head down on your shoulder; if you always carry him cradled in your arms like a small baby he will develop a tendency to curl into a ball.

For as long as your child is small enough to manage it, you should carry him in as many different ways as possible – sometimes upright (against either shoulder, not always the same one), sometimes in a sitting position, sometimes with his back to you, sometimes laying back in your arms. The position for carrying can also help with the development of the child's muscle tone.

If he is stiff, with a tendency to cross his legs, cradling him in your arms or holding him upright will encourage this and may even cause him to arch backwards, whereas holding him astride your hip with your arm across the middle of his back will help to keep his legs apart, his hips in a good position, his body flexed and make it easier for him to hold his head up.

For a child who is floppy, holding him against your shoulder or lying in your arms will give him total support, so he needs to make no effort himself, but by turning him around so that he faces away from you and holding him with your arm across his middle, allowing his arms and legs to dangle, you will encourage him to firm up and develop head control.

The final consideration for position is in respect of sleeping. During the course of the night, the average young child will turn over many times, so that when you go in to check him you are never sure whether you will find him on his front, his back, his side or even with his feet on the pillow. Indeed, the reason that toddlers often sleep in beds with sides attached is not to keep them in their bed, but more to prevent them from falling out while they are sleeping.

However, if a child has little or no voluntary movement he will be unable to turn himself over during the night and when you consider that many children sleep for eight hours or more that is a long time to remain in the same position, especially for a child who has a tendency to stiffness.

This can be problematic in two ways. Firstly, he is likely to become uncomfortable and may even suffer cramp in his muscles, both of which will make it difficult for him to settle into a deep sleep and so will result in disturbed nights for all of you.

Secondly, staying in the same position for prolonged periods of time – especially if each night he is put into the same position – increases the risk of him developing contractures and other deformities as he grows.

You should get into the habit of altering the way you place him – even if only slightly – each time you put him to bed. If you find that he lies well on one side but not the other, you can overcome this by putting a pillow behind him. If he lies on his back, sometimes placing a roll of foam behind his knees will allow him to lie with his legs bent as opposed to straight out, while a smaller roll behind one knee will let him bend just one leg.

If your child goes to sleep before you go to bed yourselves, gently turn him over or adjust his position during the evening and last thing, and again if you happen to get up during the night.

Although there is obviously a risk that moving him might disturb his sleep, if it is done quickly he will not fully wake up and if it happens on a regular basis he should get used to it. On the other hand, if he becomes stiff, cramped or uncomfortable from being in the same position for too long, the chances are that he will wake up anyway, only this time he will be miserable, which will make it more difficult for him to settle again, meaning that you too will be in for a long, wakeful night.

Keep things moving

From the moment of birth, babies are physically active, moving their limbs and turning their heads. Initially their movements are stiff and jerky and dressing a new-born can be a nerve-wracking experience as you try to push arms into sleeves and legs into trousers. There is often the feeling that something will break or become disjointed. As the baby gradually gains control of his movements he becomes more pliable, but if his disability results in physical inactivity, this level of flexibility may be delayed or, in some cases, not happen at all.

If your child shows any sign of stiffness, or if he is floppy but makes little or no voluntary movement of his own, it is important that you take his limbs through a full range of movement on a regular basis. This will not only help to keep his joints supple but will also stimulate muscle tone, discourage the development of contractures and positional deformities, allow the child to fully stretch out and let him experience good patterns of movement.

The movements should not be forced, jerky or carried out at speed but should be done in a gentle, relaxed way, never pushing beyond any restriction encountered and talking to your child at the same time.

The best place to work with the child is on a mat on the floor, or on a table, with him lying on his back. Holding around his forearm with one hand and his hand with the other, gently rotate his wrist in both directions, trying at the same time to keep his fingers open. If his arms are generally stiff and kept in a bent position, support him under the elbow and, holding around his wrist, gently rotate the lower arm, stretching it as much as possible on the downward movement.

Next, raise his arm above his head and then gently swing it out to the side and down, in a windmill-type action, before switching to the other arm and repeating the same procedures.

Moving to his legs, with his knee bent grasp his foot and bend it first so that his toes point up towards his knee then the opposite way so that they point downwards, following with a circular rotation in both directions. Next, bend his knee high towards his tummy, keeping the other leg straight, then move it gently out to the side and back again before returning it to the straight position and repeating all the movements on the other side.

Finally, gently turn his head from side to side, rotating it on its axis so that the back of your hand lands on the same spot on the mat or table each time.

As well as moving the limbs individually, you should also move them in conjunction with each other, to allow your child to experience total body movement. Raise both arms above his head at the same time, then return them to his sides, sometimes in a straight down movement and sometimes swinging them out to the sides. Bend both knees up to his tummy then straighten his legs out again, or bend them alternately in a marching action. Gently roll him first onto one side and then the other.

If you have somebody with you, you can work together to involve more of his body. With one person moving his arms and the other his legs, first stretch him out, with his arms above his head and his legs down straight, then fold him, with his knees up to his tummy and his arms by his sides. Repeat these actions several times in a rhythmical manner. This enables him to feel the contrast between stretching and curling up, which is one of the first co-ordinated movements a baby makes.

Similarly, one person can turn his head to one side while the other person raises the arm on that side so that his hand is in front of his face, repeating the movements in the opposite direction.

None of these little exercises need to be carried out for long, but they should be repeated frequently. A few minutes three or four times a day will not put a tremendous strain on your schedule but it could be enough to make a significant difference to your child's future physical condition and development.

Choose equipment carefully

The day-to-day equipment you use for your child – pushchairs, high-chairs, car-seats, etc – can play a large part in your child's physical condition and development.

If your child is to be put into a sitting position before he is able to sit independently, it is important that his spine is given adequate support and that he is not allowed to slump.

Many of today's pushchairs keep the child in a permanent sitting position, even when the seat is tilted back, which means that the spine is permanently curved, even when the child is sleeping.

The importance has already been stressed of lying the child flat, especially in the early stages, when his muscle tone is still developing, and pushchairs are readily available which allow this, usually described in their literature as having a 'lie-flat option'.

Unfortunately, the increasingly popular lightweight buggy-style can encourage the child to assume a curved semi-sitting position at all times, even when lifted up, and is so best avoided for the young disabled child.

Another factor to bear in mind when looking at seating arrangements is what happens to the child's feet.

Whereas a small baby's legs and feet are usually supported by the seat itself, as the child grows this support is naturally reduced to thigh level, leaving the lower legs to dangle over the edge of the seat. If the child is not fully upright, this puts increased strain on the spine, which as well as not being beneficial can also be very uncomfortable, and if he has a tendency towards spasticity it can encourage him to go into spasm.

You should therefore look for a pushchair that has a footrest, preferably one that is adjustable so that the height can be altered as the child grows, in order to maintain a close to ninety degree angle at both knees and ankles and allowing it to be raised to horizontal when he is lying down. The backrest should also have as many variable positions as possible, so that he can be raised in sitting just to the level that his spine is still supported and he doesn't slump or curve to the side. Another feature to look for is a five-point harness, which will help prevent the child from sliding down when in a semi-sitting position.

Footrests are also beneficial on high chairs, and the seat itself should encourage the child to sit upright rather than slouched or leaning to the side. For children with poor head control and upper body support, feeding can often be best achieved in a reclining position in a pushchair, car seat or stabilised bouncer chair, all of which can keep the head and neck properly aligned with the spine. Swallowing is extremely difficult if the head hangs back or drops forward and eating while lying flat can result in choking, whereas a supported reclining position allows gravity to help in the process.

In respect of car seats, children with poor head control will benefit from one with a recline facility in order to prevent the head form hanging forward for the entire journey, and if there is no integrated footrest there should be room for the child's feet to rest on the seat of the car itself.

It goes without saying, of course, that any equipment you use for your child should carry the British Safety Standards Kite Mark, or its equivalent in other countries

Part 2: Encourage Independent Movement

The development of mobility

In an ideal world, mobility would develop in the highly structured way of rolling from back to front and vice-versa, followed by crawling, first on the tummy, then on all fours, before pulling to stand, cruising round furniture and, finally, independent walking.

We say that this would be the ideal way because during each of these stages important development is also taking place in other areas, such as vision, hearing, comprehension, speech and hand function, all of which interact together to enable the child to progress through the various levels. (How to encourage the development of other functions will be dealt with in other chapters.)

However, as we all know, we do not live in an ideal world and many children do not follow this developmental path, usually without any apparent detriment to their functional abilities. In the case of a disabled child, though, whilst parents are naturally delighted to see their child on his feet like any other, we would strongly recommend that if he has not reached this level by a progression through the other stages, he should be encouraged to 'fill in the gaps' in order to give him the best possible chance of all-round development.

Give your child opportunity to move

As has been said earlier, your child will not be able to learn about moving first his limbs and then his body if he is always held or propped into a sitting position. Before he can reach the stage of being able to propel himself across the floor, he must first learn how to move his arms and legs individually and this is a process which, even in babies without disability, is a gradual one.

When a small baby first waves his arms about and kicks his legs, these movements are not planned and controlled but are entirely random in nature, and are totally aimless. It is only by frequent repetition, and the fact that from time to time his hands or feet will accidentally come into contact with something, that he will begin to learn how to control the movements and make them more purposeful.

As well as giving your child regular opportunities for learning about moving his limbs, you must also make it possible for him to learn how to put these movements to use in a purposeful way in order to propel himself forward.

The first and most obvious requirement is that the child needs to be put onto his tummy. In this position, although the waving of his arms and kicking of his legs will still be random and aimless, his limbs will occasionally make contact with the floor or mat and, as he gains strength, these movements will cause him to move marginally forward.

It is the constant repetition of these accidental movements which eventually leads to purposeful movement.

Once your child has achieved independent mobility at any level – whether it be commando-crawling, rolling, bottom-shuffling, crawling or indeed walking – which some children do having missed out all the previous stages – it is a question of then creating as many opportunities as possible for further levels of development.

For instance, if he is able to walk by holding on to furniture but is reluctant to let go, preferring to revert to crawling or bottom shuffling to cross an open space, reduce the gaps by rearranging your furniture so that he only needs to take two or three independent steps, gradually widening it again as he gains confidence.

If, on the other hand, he can walk but has no idea about crawling, create opportunities for this by arranging coffee tables and dining chairs in a close group and putting something he wants on the floor in the middle, so that he has to go under them to retrieve it. This can also work for a bottom-shuffler who you would like to see crawling.

Make it easy for your child to move

For children with a physical disability, trying to move can be extremely difficult and they will often give up making an effort because they do not appear to be achieving anything. It is therefore essential that wherever possible you create situations which make it easier for your child to succeed.

This can be done most effectively simply by looking at how you dress your child and the surface you put him on, in relation to the movements you are hoping he will achieve. For example, if you are encouraging him to move forwards on his tummy you should put him down on a smooth surface – cushion floor, cork, lino, wood block, etc, and dress him in shorts and T-shirt, so that his arms and legs are bare. The reason for this is quite simple – the body is the heaviest part of the child, and needs to be able to slide smoothly whilst the limbs, which are often lacking in strength, need to be able to grip the surface in order to propel the body forward.

Putting the child onto a carpet, blanket, etc, totally reverses this situation – the weight of his body pushes down onto the surface so that his clothing grips tight and his arms and legs are not strong enough to move him. Similarly, putting him onto a smooth surface wearing long trousers and long sleeves will also render him immobile, this time because the clothing on his limbs will skim over the surface, preventing him from getting a grip in order to push or pull himself along.

In addition to this, if your child constantly dribbles and is unable to lift his head when lying face down, you will need to place a cloth under his cheek, as the wetness will cause his face to stick to the surface, acting as a very effective brake.

A very simple aid to initiating independent forward movement on the tummy is to place the child on an inclined surface. This can be achieved either by the use of a purpose-built, wide, wooden ramp, with sides and adjustable height, or more simply by using a long piece of smooth wood or hardboard (an unused flat door would suffice) covered with something such as cushion floor and placing one end on blocks or bricks to create the incline. (Obviously, if there are no sides to the ramp you should ensure that there is always somebody standing by the child to reposition if necessary to prevent him falling off!).

When the child is placed on his tummy on a sloping surface, head towards the bottom, gravity will assist him, so that movement of his arms and legs, or in some cases simply wriggling his body, which achieve nothing when he is on the floor, will cause him to slide down a little, enabling him to learn about cause and effect.

The height of the slope should be such that if he lies still he stays put – i.e. he doesn't simply slide down from one kick, in which case it is too high – but if he moves his limbs vigorously he doesn't remain in the same place, which would indicate that it is too low.

When he reaches the bottom you should pick him up, make a big fuss and tell him how clever he is before putting him back to try again. Over a period of time, as he gains speed and his movements become more co-ordinated, reduce the height by a fraction so that he has to work a little harder to achieve the same result – but not so much that it becomes too difficult or he will simply give up.

If, on the other hand, your child can already commando crawl and you are trying to encourage the next level of crawling on hands and knees, a carpet is a better surface to put him on, wearing long trousers. This will enable him to gain some traction with his knees, whereas on a smooth surface he would have a tendency to slide around, causing his knees to splay out.

Also, if he does overbalance or his arms give out – both of which are likely to happen a few times – a carpet is a friendlier surface to land on. Incidentally, the clothing described applies just as much to little girls as to boys – dresses and skirts are a total inhibitor to movement. All that happens is that limbs get tangled up in material and the child nearly chokes herself as she tries to move forward.

When you are at the stage of encouraging your child to take independent steps, footwear is the important factor. Ideally, he should be either barefoot or wearing shoes <u>and</u> socks – never just in socks. The problem with them is twofold – first of all, if he happens to step onto a smooth surface he is likely to slip, which as well as shaking his confidence could actually cause him injury if he fell heavily or did the splits, and secondly, socks have a habit of riding down, leaving the toe section empty to flap around, which can easily cause him to trip up.

At this stage, you should also look carefully at furniture, etc, in the rooms that the child uses, making sure that any sharp corners and edges are protected with foam or something similar, bearing in mind that a disabled child is often starting to walk at a later age than usual and so will be taller and thus have further to fall.

Give your child a reason to move

Because movement is often extremely hard work for a disabled child, his motivation to move must be very high in order to justify making the effort. He is unlikely to find movement pleasurable in itself and will quickly give up if he sees no reason, purpose or reward, so you need to continually look for incentives that will encourage him to make the required effort. A few ideas of how this can be achieved to start you off are given, but your child will probably soon became bored with them, and it is then up to you to work out the nature of reward that provides the highest level of motivation for him.

If your child has little or no voluntary movement of his limbs and you are trying to encourage him to wave his arms and kick his legs, you can help by stitching little bells onto sweatbands or covered pony tail elastics and slipping them onto his wrists and ankles, so that any little movement he makes will produce a sound which will, hopefully, stimulate him to repeat it.

Alternatively, you could suspend lightweight objects – that either make a sound or reflect light when moved – on string, so that when he moves his limbs he will knock them, again causing an effect that will make him want to try again. Obviously, the key to this is the position of the suspended objects – it will not work unless his hand or foot make contact as a result of the smallest movement.

Trying to encourage a child to move forward on his tummy, whether on the floor or an inclined surface, often requires a little more ingenuity, since the effort needed for this is of a more sustained nature. If he has a favourite toy, or something he especially likes to look at, put it just out of reach (some children are more likely to make the effort for food or chocolate!)

It is no use leaving a large space between him and his target, he will see that as being unattainable and not even begin to try. The goal he is aiming for needs to be placed so that even when he stretches out fully he can't quite reach it, but if he lurches forward – either by pulling with his arm or pushing with a leg – it comes within grasping distance.

Only as he becomes able to achieve this on a consistent basis should you start to gradually extend the space you want him to cover.

If your child has additional problems that include a lack of vision, you should also bear in mind that he probably has no way of knowing that the spot 12 inches in front of him is any different from the one on which he is currently lying, so in this case he needs to be coaxed forward towards a voice or noisy toy and rewarded with a cuddle or some other form of physical contact as soon as a movement has been accomplished.

If your child has developed the ability to move forward but is reluctant to put it to use, the targets need to be a little more imaginative. For instance, if he dislikes being excluded from the family group, or objects to having you out of his sight, try putting him just outside the door or round a corner so that he can hear you but not see you. Carry on with whatever you are doing, but occasionally call out to him, reminding him that you know he is still there and want him to join you.

Don't make the mistake of keep popping out to see him, all that will happen then is that he will lie and wait for your next appearance or, even worse, will simply cry for you to go to him.

He needs to learn that if he wants to be with you he must make the effort himself – and do be sure to pile on the praise and encouragement when he comes into view.

If he has some level of comprehension, you can also try giving specific rewards to aim for – for example, when he reaches the television you will put on his favourite video, or when he gets to Daddy he will pick him up and swing him into the air.

This will, of course, only work if the reward is withheld if he does not reach his goal – if he knows it will be given anyway, why should he bother to make the effort?

Give assistance where necessary

Although it is important that your child is given opportunities and encouragement to move by himself, you need to recognise situations where just a little physical help from you would make it possible for him to achieve his goal.

If he is trying to hit a dangling object but going into spasm, try gently raising his arm just by placing your finger under his elbow so that he is able to make the initial contact.

If, when he is on his tummy, he is making desperate attempts to move forward but going nowhere, wait until he bends one of his legs then quickly put your hand behind his foot so that he has something to push against – and as long as you remember to keep your hand still, his normal kicking action will cause him to shoot forward.

Alternatively, if he seems to be trying to drag himself forward with his arms but is unable to get a grip, when he reaches forward put your hands over his and press them firmly down – don't hold his hands or let him hold yours, you are helping him to understand the need to pull against the surface of the floor, not against you. By doing this, when he tries to drag himself along you will prevent his arms from skimming back towards him, so that his body will then move forwards.

If your child can get up onto his hands and knees but is then unable to move, you can assist him by placing your hand under his chest and gently lifting, not to the point that his hands come off the floor but just sufficiently to take the weight off them so that he is able to move one forward – if he is reluctant, try tickling the inside of his wrist. Alternatively, you can grasp him firmly round the rib cage and slowly ease his weight forward over his hands so that he feels off balance, hopefully triggering his 'saving reflex' to make him reach forward. (It is important to hold firmly to prevent him from taking a nose dive if he fails to move his hand.)

For many children, the stage between walking round furniture, or holding an adult's hand and taking independent steps, seems to last forever, the child appearing to be on the verge of walking for a long time. There are several ways in which you can encourage him on to the next stage.

If he is quite confident to stand with just a little support, place him with his back to a wall and kneel or crouch in front of him with a distance of no more than 2 or 3 steps between you. Put your hands in front of you, palms up, and encourage him to come to you – but don't reach out to him, this will only prompt him to grab. If he is hesitant, lightly hold the front of his jumper and gently pull him towards you, just so that his back moves away from the wall – being careful not to bring him too far forward or he will simply fall over.

Letting him walk away from a wall rather than starting him off yourself means that he has the opportunity to sort his balance out himself, so that he feels steady before lifting his foot. If he is happy to walk just holding onto your finger but either sits down or grabs you as soon as he feels that you are trying to remove the support, get him to hold onto a short dowel instead, with you holding the other end – you may then find that as he is walking you can let go of the dowel without him realising and he will simply carry on, as long as he still has something to cling to.

A stage up from this is to replace the dowel with a short piece of strong rope – this will be far less stable and will constantly move, which will result in the child having to rely on his own balance to stay upright as well as taking steps forward.

If there are two of you, stand facing each other just a few steps apart, with the person behind the child supporting him at the hips. Wait until you can feel that he is fully balanced and not leaning on you, then start to slowly walk forwards with the other person walking backwards at the same rate. After a couple of steps, let go of him, but keep your arms on either side in case he topples over. You must, of course, increase your speed of movement to match his if he suddenly takes off – the objective is for the person he is walking towards to remain the same distance from him so that he doesn't realise how far he is travelling.

Stimulate your child's balance

No child is born with a sense of balance, this is something that develops as the child is handled, moved around through different positions and eventually learns to move himself, alongside the maturation of his sight and hearing.

Many times during the day, the baby is lifted from lying in his cot or pram into his parent's arms and put down again. Each time this happens he momentarily travels through space at some speed in relation to his size and weight. Each time he is lifted and held upright against Mum's shoulder his position changes quite quickly from horizontal to vertical, and vice-versa when he is placed back in his cot. When he learns to roll over, the action of turning from his back to his tummy and then in the other direction is repeated regularly, giving him frequent, rapid changes of position in space.

Before starting to crawl on all fours, most babies get up onto their hands and knees and spend time rocking backwards and forwards. This helps them to learn about balancing by shifting their weight from arms to legs and back again so that when they eventually lift a hand to move forward they do not fall over.

It is usually around this stage that parents start to play with their baby by swinging him up into the air, holding him upside down, twirling him round etc, giving him yet more experiences of his body moving through space. (All of these activities are also equally important for other areas of development but are often sadly lacking from the life of a disabled child. This is covered in more detail in the section relating to social development.)

When the child becomes properly mobile, his own movements and activities continue to provide even more feedback and stimulation in respect of balance as he learns to walk and run, climbs onto and over things, bends down and stands up again, momentarily stands on one foot when dressing – the list is endless. Children also have an in-built desire to put themselves upside down, and you have almost certainly seen them hanging over the edge of a chair or couch to read a book, swinging upside down with their knees over a rail or the branch of a tree, or standing on their heads. Even toddlers can be seen bending double to look back between their feet. They do not carry out these activities just because they enjoy them, it is all part of our inherited patterns of learning which encourage the process of development.

Parents of children with disabilities often develop a tendency to 'wrap them in cotton wool' and are reluctant to handle them as "roughly" as they would their other children. While this is quite understandable, they are, in fact, depriving their child of many vital experiences of movement through space which are essential for the development of balance and mobility. In addition to this, if the child has little voluntary or independent movement, he is unable to carry out any of the activities that would normally provide his brain with further information about balance, so that, in effect, you have a chicken-and-egg situation – restricted movement hinders the development of balance and an inability to balance makes it more difficult to learn about movement.

You can, however, help to stimulate the development of your child's balance by making sure that you give him different experiences of moving through space as frequently as possible.

This could be by swinging him, backwards and forwards and from side to side – either by holding him in your arms or with two people grasping him, either by his wrists and ankles or by the corners of a blanket he is lying on, or simply in a baby swing.

You could move him swiftly from horizontal to upright several times or roll him back and forth from tummy to back. You could let him hang upside down for a few seconds, either from sitting on your knee or by holding him round his ankles or over the edge of a chair – making sure, of course, that you maintain a strong grip of him and that he is only in the position briefly.

In other words, watch other small children playing and think back to what his brothers and sisters may have done, and try wherever possible to reproduce the same experiences and sensations for your disabled child.

As well as helping his development, it should also prove to be fun for all of you.

4. Encouraging Intellectual Development

There seems to be a commonly held belief that intelligence is measured by speech – that in order to prove that you can understand what is being said you must be able to answer questions and express yourself verbally.

This is, in fact, little more than a myth.

Many children, and indeed adults, whose physical disabilities make them unable to produce meaningful vocalisation or control a pencil are nonetheless capable of high academic achievements.

This is clearly illustrated in the case of a hypothetical stroke victim, who overnight has lost the use of a hand and the power of speech. Are we to assume that he has suddenly lost all the knowledge he has acquired during his life, along with the ability to think and to understand what we are saying to him? Of course not. In fact, we go to great lengths to reassure him that we know he understands us, that his inability to express himself is a result of the stroke and that, hopefully, given time he will recover some, if not all, of his functions. Why, then, are we so reluctant to accept that a young disabled child who cannot speak to us might nevertheless be capable of comprehending everything we say to him? This is surely a reflection of our own intellectual limitations rather than his.

A second myth regarding the development of intelligence is that we either have it or we don't – that our genetic inheritance wholly dictates whether we are smart or dumb and little can be done to change the situation. Whilst, undoubtedly, nature does play a large part in our ability to achieve, we are equally affected by our environment, the attitudes of others to us, the opportunities given to us and the expectations made of us.

No baby is born with an inbuilt ability to understand, this develops over time as a result of interaction with the adults around him, the continual repetition of sounds and events and the gradual realisation of cause and effect.

At birth, the baby is a blank canvas and the picture that will slowly evolve will depend very much on the richness and variety of the 'materials' used – in other words, the input from those caring for him.

An easy way to illustrate how the ability to comprehend language develops is to imagine three babies, identical triplets born in Britain to an English mother and an Italian father. Immediately after birth circumstances dictate that the babies are separated: one stays with his parents, one is brought up by his totally English grandparents and the third is sent to live in Italy with relatives who speak only in their native tongue.

Three or four years later, a great family reunion in England brings the children into contact with each other for the first time since birth. The adults excitedly compare notes and are satisfied that all three boys have attained the same levels of ability in most areas. (For the purpose of this illustration we must assume that all three babies are given the same attention and stimulation, the same opportunities and achieve all their milestones at a similar age.)

Attention is then turned to the children themselves, all of whom are eager to talk. The child living with the English grandparents is happy enough, since the majority of people in the room speak the same language as him and they in turn respond to his conversation. The boy who has been living in Italy becomes increasingly reticent when he realises that only a handful of people besides his grandparents appear to understand what he says and that he, in turn, has little idea of what is being asked of him. The third triplet, on the other hand, is relaxed, outgoing and extremely comfortable with the situation. Not only can he switch effortlessly between the two languages, making it possible to communicate with all present, but he also quickly takes the lead in the children's activities, acting as mediator and translator.

On the face of it, an onlooker might assume that this third child was far more intelligent than the others, being fluent in two languages, while the child from Italy might seem a little "dull" in comparison with his more outgoing English-speaking brother.

Of course, the perception of these two boys would be reversed if the reunion took place in Italy, but with the bi-lingual brother still appearing to be the "brightest".

In reality, however, there is no difference whatsoever between the boys in terms of their intelligence or their ability to learn – merely in the environment they had been exposed to.

Part 1: Input of Information

Stimulate the senses

From the day they are born, babies start to learn, taking in information about the world around them through all their senses – seeing, hearing, feeling, tasting and smelling.

Initially this is a very passive process, with stimulus reaching the baby almost by accident, but gradually, as things become more meaningful, he will actively seek out new stimulation to enhance the learning process – looking with interest at something bright and moving, becoming fascinated by the sound of a musical toy, reaching out to touch a furry toy or taking everything he picks up to his mouth. This is something most babies will do naturally, but if the child has some degree of disability – whether from birth or acquired later in life following illness or traumatic injury – you may actually need to be provide the experiences for him to start the learning process at a very basic level.

Vision

Make sure that whenever your child is awake there is something close by for him to look at – he will never learn to focus his eyes if everything of interest is outside his visual field.

The things most likely to catch his attention are bright colours and shiny surface which reflect light, such as a simple mobile made from Christmas baubles suspended within 2-3 feet of his face or twinkling fairy lights clumped together – stringing them out will make the area too vast for him to focus on and he will simply ignore them.

Change the stimulus regularly, otherwise it will quickly become part of the background and of no interest. Once your child is making eye contact with you, very slowly move your face from one side to the other, across his line of vision, maintaining eye contact and talking to him all the time – this will encourage him to start to follow with his eyes. If he "loses" you, keep still and continue talking until he looks for you and resumes eye contact.

Similarly, if you find something that he particularly likes to look at, move this object slowly in all directions, gradually increasing both the range and speed of movements as he learns to control his eyes. Whenever he stops focusing on the object, bring it back to within his range of vision and encourage him to look for it.

Hearing

Before a child can develop recognition and understanding of sounds he must first learn to *listen*.

For many disabled children, the problem is not one of hearing the sound but of *attending* to it. In other words, if there is a lot of noise going on around them they can hear it all but don't pay attention to any one sound in particular – it is just chaotic noise. The result of this is often that they simply don't appear to respond when spoken to or when a sound is presented to them.

Spend time with your child encouraging him to listen. Lie next to him and gently call him, repeating his name until he turns towards you. Get his attention with a musical toy, letting him both see and hear it, then remove it from view. After distracting his attention, make the toy produce the noise out of his sight then ask him "where is it?"

Keep repeating the sound followed by the question until he appears to be making movements of his eyes or head towards the direction of the sound then let him see it.

Talk to him in different tones and volume of voice – sometimes whispering, sometimes louder, sometimes sing-song. Put together a collection of toys and objects with a wide variety of sounds and use them to attract his attention.

Touch

Many disabled children suffer from impaired sensation which limits their ability to learn from touch and can result in injury. A child with poor perception of pain, for instance, might roll against a hot radiator and not realise they are being burnt so will make no effort to roll away from it. Also, if a child cannot properly feel his arms and legs he will not be motivated to try to move them, which will impair his development of movement.

From an early age, make sure you handle your child regularly, rubbing and massaging his limbs and body, tickling him, stroking him with different textures – a piece of fur, a soft brush, a pan cleaner. Make sure you don't forget areas such as his face and neck, his back, the soles of his feet and between his fingers.

Once babies can reach out to things, they are constantly patting, stroking and grabbing with their hands, which eventually develops into purposeful hand function, but if your child's hands are closed in tight fists he will not be able to do this. Gently open his fingers and touch the palms of his hands with different objects and textures, moving and turning them so he feels shape and edges. Take his hand and stroke first his own face and then yours, letting him feel the contours of nose, lips and hair.

Taste and smell

As babies become more aware and mobile, everything they pick up is taken to their face to be explored with their mouth and nose – a phase all parents despair of! However, this is a normal and very important stage of development, rather than just an annoying habit, and helps the child compile more information about the world around him.

While he is rolling and crawling around the floor and handling different objects he is continually coming into contact with different tastes and smells, but the child who has no mobility and can't effectively pick things up loses out on this experience.

Also, at this age, the baby is usually progressing to more variety of taste and texture in his food, whereas many disabled babies are on a very bland and smooth diet. You can, however, provide opportunities to help your child to learn through taste and smell. When you have been helping him to feel an object with his hand, take it to his mouth and move it gently across his lips and tongue. Help him to put his own thumb and fingers into his mouth and move them around so he feels his gums, tongue and the inside of his cheeks. Make sure he also experiences different flavours of food and drink – even a child fed by tubes can cope with a tiny drop of something sweet, sour or bitter placed directly on the tongue with a dropper or rubbed across his lips. Stimulation from taste and texture is essential to produce the movements of mouth and tongue necessary for good feeding and, eventually, speech.

Combining the senses

Whilst it is important to make sure that each of the senses is stimulated individually, children learn little in isolation. You therefore need to make sure that you show your child how to combine what he experiences through his eyes, ears, hands and mouth to form a more complete impression. For example, find a toy or object that is brightly coloured and makes a noise and hold it in front of his face, encouraging him to look at it. When you are sure he has seen it, shake it so that it produces a sound, again encouraging him verbally to listen.

Next, take one or both of his hands and allow him to feel the surface of the object, paying attention to curves and edges, before finally helping him to hold it and take it to his mouth. In this way you are reproducing a pattern of behaviour which babies without disability perform countless times a day.

Provide contrasts

If your child has major problems in the areas of sight, hearing or sensation due to an injury in the brain rather than damage or defect to the organ itself, you can encourage him to look and listen by increasing the contrast of the stimulus you are providing.

For example, it might be very difficult for him to focus on a coloured, flickering light in a normally-lit room with lots of other things around to distract him – he probably won't even be aware that it is there, it will simply merge into the background. However, if before asking him to look you completely darken the room – or, even better, take him into a dark cupboard under the stairs – the contrast when the light is switched on will make it much easier for him to focus his attention.

Similarly, when trying to get your child to respond to the sound of a musical toy or rattle, first have a few seconds of total silence so that the noise will be easier to hear.

What you are doing is providing a filtering process, which highlights the thing you want him to concentrate on and removes all incidental distractions.

Contrasts can also be used to improve sensation. Stroking his limbs with first a rough texture, such as a pan cleaner or comb, then immediately afterwards with a piece of soft fur or smooth velvet, or with a hot flannel followed by an icy cold one, will make him more aware of what he is feeling.

Vary the direction of stimulus

In chapter two, the importance of changing your child's position in order to avoid deformity and restricted movement was covered. In the same way, it is important for the development of vision and hearing. For example, if the baby's cot is against a wall he will continually turn his head away if he wants to see something other than a blank wall and might eventually form a habit of only looking in one direction. The ideal position for the cot would be in the middle of the room, with things to look at on either side, but if space restrictions mean that it has to be against a wall at least change the direction you lie the baby in – sometimes with his head to one end and sometimes to the other.

If you are holding him and making eye contact as you talk or play, sometimes hold him in your left arm, sometimes in the right and other times facing you. If he is lying on his back, approach him one time from below his chin and another from above his head. In this way he will learn to look up and down as well as from side to side. Making sure that he looks at things in all directions will encourage the use of both eyes independently and help them develop equally, which is essential for good binocular vision. Similarly, sounds should be presented to the child from a variety of directions, both in respect of noisy toys and people talking to him.

You should also vary the child's position within the room. If he sits in his own seat, move it around from place to place, or if you put him on ordinary furniture, change him from seat to seat. Always sitting in the same place will result in him always seeing and hearing the television from the same direction, always viewing items within the room from the same angle and always knowing exactly where he will be. How many young children without disabilities do you know who stay in one place for more than a short time?

Talk to your child

If you were to find yourself in a position of being able to do only one thing for your disabled baby this would be the single most important in terms of his intellectual development. Intelligence in humans revolves around language, whether it be in the spoken or written form, and without the comprehension of language it is nigh on impossible to demonstrate intellectual ability.

However, children are not born with any pre-installed language – it is something that must be taught and cultivated by those around them as they grow and learn.

The vast majority of parents do not consciously set out to teach their child language, it is something that evolves as the baby becomes responsive and more assertive. Body parts, for example, are usually learned by frequent reference to them during everyday activities such as washing, dressing, feeding etc – 'let's wipe your face', 'put it over your head', 'open your mouth', 'give me your hand', etc. Names of objects and people often accompany statements such as 'here's teddy', 'hold your bottle', 'go to Daddy', 'let's put you in your highchair', 'time for a bath', etc. Verbs are commonly learned by hearing negative instructions like 'don't touch', 'get down', 'stop screaming' and in simple activities such as 'clap hands', 'give it to me', 'kiss teddy'.

As the baby becomes more mobile and starts to move around and explore his environment the vocabulary of words he understands also grows as he hears instructions such as 'come away from the television', 'don't climb on the chair', 'the fire is hot', 'put the paper down'. He doesn't comprehend the full sentence or even necessarily the gist of what is being said, but key words will become familiar, especially if he hears them in different contexts – for example if he is told at various times 'here's teddy', 'kiss teddy', 'put teddy down', 'don't hit teddy', 'where's teddy's nose' he might not understand all the instructions but he will quickly learn that his favourite cuddly toy is called Teddy.

Get into the habit right from the start of telling your child everything that you are doing with him – 'it's time to get up', 'let's get you dressed', 'I'm going to put your bib on, then you can have breakfast', etc, etc. In other words, provide him with a running commentary of what is going on. Of course, he won't understand any of it at the beginning, but it will establish communication between you. He will become very familiar with the sound and inflections of your voice and will listen to the rhythms and tones of what you are saying – and since many of his routines will be repetitive in nature, he will gradually come to associate particular words or phrases with specific activities. It will also have the added bonus of giving you something to say. Many parents confess to not talking enough to their disabled baby because they feel silly or don't know what to talk about.

Introduce your child to books

Books can play an important role in any child's life, but especially for a chid with disabilities. Not only are they an excellent way of expanding your child's vocabulary and developing imagination by describing situations normally inaccessible to him, they can also provide quality 'together time' for a disabled child and a parent who is less comfortable talking in an abstract way or playing with a child with limited responses.

Don't think your baby is too young to be introduced to books. If he is able to focus his eyes on an object, he is able to look at a picture in a book. Settle yourself in a comfortable position with the child on your lap or well supported by your side and hold the book facing you both.

Begin with simple picture books with one item per page and simply tell him the name of each item, touching or pointing to it at the same time. As soon as you think he has seen it, move on to the next page – you are not trying to get him to study it, you just want to catch his attention and let him hear the word as he sees the object.

At this stage, his attention span is not long enough to let him keep on looking at the same page, he will simply lose interest.

Similarly, don't expect him to be happy to sit and look at books for a lengthy period of time; keep the sessions short and stop while he is still happy – a few minutes two or three times a day will be more meaningful than one full hour and the child will be more likely to look forward to this special one-to-one time with keen anticipation.

Once you have established that your child is happy to sit and look at books with you, and that he does seem to be paying some visual attention, start to draw his attention to different aspects of the picture. If it is a dog, for instance, point to the head, eyes, legs and tail. If it's a ball, trace your finger around the outline and introduce the word "round". Point out different colours, show him that a car has wheels – in other words make him aware of detail within the picture.

Move on to more complex pictures, which have more than a single object or a scene depicting some activity and describe to him what is going on – the boy is kicking the ball, the cat is drinking the milk, the children are playing in the park.

When you have reached the stage of feeling comfortable with these book sessions, you are ready to look for books which tell a simple story – mainly through pictures, with a written sentence or two on each page.

Read the story to your child, pointing to the relevant parts of the picture and adding any additional comments you think might help him to understand what is going on. Use different tone of voice and inflection to emphasise emotion, surprise, amusement, etc and to personalise individual characters so that even if he doesn't fully understand the language he will find the story entertaining and look forward to the next time round.

Young children thrive on repetition and each time you read the story together he will understand and remember a little more than the last time. As you introduce a wider variety of books you will find that you can easily tell which ones are his favourites, the ones he wants you to read time and time again – and, by the way, this applies to *all* children, not only those with disabilities.

Not only can books play a significant part in helping your child to understand language, they can provide opportunities for spending meaningful time together and helping you to develop communication and shared interests.

Part 2: Opportunities for Output

Help your child to explore his environment

Once a baby becomes independently mobile, it becomes more and more difficult to contain him in one place as he develops curiosity. What is at the other side of the room? Where does that door lead to? Who is in the kitchen? How does this drawer open?

As he gets older, he moves around the house freely, going in and out of rooms at will, seeing who is where and what they are doing. For a child who can't move around, however, exploring his environment is not an option – unless, that is, you help him to do it.

Make sure your child is familiar with the layout of your house. Take him in and out of all the rooms on a regular basis. If an older sister is in her bedroom playing or listening to music, say to your disabled child, "Let's go and see what she is doing…" If his father is in the garage or out in the shed, say, "Where's daddy gone? Shall we go and find him?" and make a point of looking in several places before happening on the right one. If you hear a motorbike or heavy lorry go by, say, "I wonder what that is?" and take him to the window to see. These are things a lively, inquisitive child would be doing naturally, and your child with disabilities might just be longing to do the same.

It is also important for your child to explore the individual rooms themselves, not only to learn about the contents, but also such things as corners – to a child who is always in the same place, a corner can appear like a flat wall, without dimension. Take him around the room, giving the names of things in a conversational way as you go – "Let's put this lamp in the corner." "That's a nice picture of Grandma." "What's inside this drawer?"

As well as his immediate surroundings, be sure to let him become aware of the wider environment outside his home. While you might be content staying on the paths in the park, an energetic five-year-old will be running all over the place – going round trees, looking through fences, investigating puddles.

Taking your disabled five-year-old to the park in his wheelchair might, in itself, be a nice little outing, but you could make it more exciting and create opportunities for learning by venturing off the paths and into less obvious places – even if they are a little more difficult to access. Similarly, on a visit to friends or relatives, ask if you might show your child around at least the downstairs area – after all, if he weren't disabled he would be investigating of his own accord!

Anticipate his questions

As children acquire language, their curiosity begins to escalate. No longer are they content with who, what and where, they now want to know how and why. We are all familiar with the endless stream of questions posed by a young chatterbox – some of which we might find difficult to answer, such as "why is the sky blue?" but this is how children learn about and begin to interact with the world around them. If your child can't speak or has difficulty in communicating his thoughts, this information will not be available to him unless you are aware of what a child at his stage of development would want to know, and provide the answers without the questions being asked.

The first question asked by most young children is "what" as they point to things outside their experience, asking "what's that?". If your child has little or no speech, you should try to be aware of when he is coming into contact with something he has not seen before and provide him with its name in a very matter-of-fact way, gradually increasing his vocabulary.

The next question is usually "where" as in "Where's Daddy?" or "Where are you going?". Try wherever possible to recognise situations where these questions may arise and provide the answers automatically – during the day tell him that "Daddy will be home later, he's at work now" or instead of just leaving the room say "I'm going to the kitchen, I'll be back in a minute".

The question from children which causes the biggest headache for all adults is "why" followed by the equally difficult question of "how" – these questions seem to go on forever until, in sheer exasperation, you hear yourself giving such inadequate responses as "because it is!" or "because I said so!"

These questions hit us hard because they require a lot more thought and we often feel incapable of offering a satisfactory answer, so it is not surprising that we find ourselves putting off or avoiding situations where they might arise.

However, they are a vital part of the learning process and if the child is unable to ask for the information they are seeking it is down to you to recognise opportunities for providing it.

For example, instead of just changing your child's position, tell him, "I'm putting you in your chair because it's nearly dinner time" or, if his sister is crying, explain that "she is upset because her doll has been broken".

Similarly, with 'how', show him that "you make this toy move by pushing this button" or "I made that noise by blowing this whistle".

Anticipating questions and answering them is merely an extension of providing a running commentary, as discussed earlier in this chapter, only now you need to apply more in-depth consideration to the nature and quality of the information you are providing. The more you talk to your child about the whats, wheres, whys and hows, the more curious and inquisitive he will become, which will eventually lead to him being able to deduce his own answers based on the information he has previously acquired.

Learn to recognise his responses

As a baby develops personality, it is relatively easy to learn his likes and dislikes. He will clearly show his displeasure by facial expression, vocalisation, body language and temper tantrums. Similarly, when something pleases him it will be evident by his smiles, squeals, laughter and excited flapping of arms and legs.

In the same way, most parents become quite adept at recognising when their baby is hungry, tired, in pain or just fed up by the differing sound of their cry.

A baby with a disability, however, might show some delay in developing the ability to smile, make eye contact and move his limbs, which in turn will delay his ability to respond to different activities and situations. This does not mean that he isn't able to experience pleasure, discomfort or irritation, it simply means that, as yet, he is unable to make you aware of his feelings. If you are to establish a real bond with your baby, it is very important that you observe him closely and watch for signs that he might, in his own way, be responding to a given situation.

This response might take the form of a slight change of facial expression, an increase or decrease in the rate of his breathing, an opening or closing of his eyes, a particular way of wriggling his body or any other unique action or change to his usual state.

I have known many parents who can say with confidence such things as, "I know he likes a particular song because he always opens his eyes wide" or "he doesn't like to be in the dark, I can tell by the way he makes his legs go very stiff". By careful watching and monitoring, you will gradually learn not only what your child likes and dislikes but also how he is choosing to let you know. Make sure that as soon as you have some understanding of this you communicate to him, by both words and actions, that you are aware of his efforts to respond. If you don't, he will soon learn that there is no point in trying, because nobody is taking any notice.

As babies grow into toddlers and young children, we start to ask them questions – Do you want? Do you like? What's this? Who is that? etc.

Most, if not all of us, are tuned into expecting a verbal response or a gesture, such as pointing, but again, if your child is disabled these modes of response might simply be beyond him, so it is up to you to establish some other means of communication.

This might take the form of basic vocalisation – a grunt for yes, silence for no – or something more physical in nature. If the child has very little movement, he might indicate a positive response by raising his arm or opening his hand, while closing his fist could mean a negative response. On the other hand, a child with excessive involuntary movement would find movement of his limbs difficult to control, so for him it might be easier to look up towards the ceiling for yes and close his eyes for no.

Other responses I have seen in use include keeping still to indicate yes and vigorous kicking of legs to say no, showing positive with a smile and negative by turning the head away, and even pushing the tongue out for no and keeping it in for yes.

It is of no consequence what signs or signals you and your child decide to adopt, what matters is that you inform everyone who has dealings with the child that this is an effective way of communicating with him and ask them to please use it at every opportunity.

Include him in conversation

One of the easiest traps to fall into when in the company of a disabled or non-communicative child is to speak *around* him and not *to* him; to hold a conversation *about* him but not *involve* him. The "does he take sugar?" syndrome is very real and quite difficult to avoid, especially for people who either don't believe the child can understand what they are saying or are afraid that if he does and he tries to answer then *they* will not understand *him*.

It is vital that you act as an intermediary in these situations, draw him into the conversation, make him feel that you at least are interested in what he thinks. If someone asks you if your child would like a drink, don't just respond automatically, turn to the child first and ask him directly.

You might still have to decide yourself and answer for him, but at least you will have given him the opportunity to make his wishes known – and others will gradually take your lead.

Once you have set up a form of communication, as outlined above, give him opportunities to use it within conversational settings.

Let him show you what he knows

Assuming that you have got to grips with talking to your child and providing him with sensory information, it is equally important to give him regular opportunities to show you what he is learning and just how much he knows. This is important for both of you for a variety of reasons.

For you, it will provide feedback that your efforts have not been in vain and will motivate you to keep on going. For your child, it will create a sense of purpose and encourage a desire to learn. For both of you, it will help develop meaningful communication between you, with the added of bonus of establishing pride in his achievements.

As a child develops speech, mobility and hand function, parents become increasingly amazed by how quickly he picks up information and works things out, without being told or shown. He will say the names of toys and people, he will pick up objects and imitate associated actions, such as brushing his hair or pretending to drink, he will perform actions to rhymes and songs and will take you by the hand to show you something that he wants but which is out of reach.

The fact that a child might be unable to vocalise his thoughts or carry out voluntary movements does not automatically mean that he is not learning from situations and processing information. It is often the case that he simply has no means of demonstrating to you how much he knows. It is therefore vital that you create opportunities for him to show you the extent of his knowledge.

You can begin at a very basic level, by holding up two objects and asking him to "look at the cup" or with a more complex question such as "which one do you drink from?"

The same process can be repeated with pictures instead of objects and, eventually, with written words, assuming that you have first taken the time to provide repeated exposure to them.

You can also test his understanding of concepts such as size, shape and colour, by selection, using a response that you both recognise, as discussed earlier.

However, when testing your child's knowledge, there are some important points to remember.

Firstly, don't expect your child to be one hundred per cent right all the time. After all, do *you* remember everything you were ever taught? And don't keep repeating the same question just because you find it difficult to believe that he knows the answer.

An unforgettable example of this was a child who was able to recognise colours but eventually faltered when asked over and over to identify the colour of a red car. In the end, she reasoned that she must be giving the wrong answer because, although she kept repeating "red", they continued to ask the same question, so she changed her response to "blue" – at which point her father declared that he was right in his suspicion that she didn't recognise colours after all!

The only person showing an inability to learn in this case was the father, who not only failed to recognise his daughter's degree of knowledge, but also the level of intuition which led her to modify her answer.

Finally, all testing situations should be engineered in such a way that they are fun, do not put the child under any pressure and are accompanied by lots of praise, so that he is eager to take part and encouraged to give you the feedback you need in order to present him with greater challenges.

Give your child choices

Once your child is demonstrating a basic understanding of some simple words, start to give him choices concerning his everyday life. For instance, if you feel it is time he had a drink, instead of just presenting him with a bottle of milk, show him two bottles or cups, one containing milk and the other juice or water. Hold them apart and ask what would he like to drink, watching closely to see if he looks or reaches towards one of them.

If he does, present that one to him, saying the appropriate word. If not, hold each one in front of him in turn, saying, "here's milk … here's juice" and then ask the question again.

If there is still no response, decide which to give him and then say, "You don't know which you want, so I'll give you …" putting the other bottle away.

In the same way, when you are dressing him, show him two different T-shirts and ask him which he wants to wear, or at bed time ask who he wants to take him, Mummy or Daddy. If you are putting him down, ask if he wants to go on the floor or in his chair. If you are sitting down with a book, let him choose which one he wants, etc, etc.

When giving your child choices, there are several factors to bear in mind. Don't offer a choice if you are not in a position to honour his selection – it's no use, for instance, asking who he wants to take him to bed if Daddy has to go out. Give the child a way of making his choice – if he can't *say* what he wants, or reach out towards it, ask him to look at it, or say the names of both and ask him to indicate yes or no each time by whatever method you have established together.

And finally, make sure that once he has made his choice he understands that he must live with what he has chosen – for the time being, at least. This is the only way he will be able to learn the true meaning of choice.

5. Encouraging Social Development

One of the most worrying thoughts for parents of a disabled child is how will he be accepted by others and integrated into society. In general, they see the biggest obstacle to this as being his condition itself, both from the point of view that it will impair his abilities to socialise and also that it will colour the attitudes of other people before they even give him a chance. Whilst these are undeniably valid points and should not be lightly disregarded, there are other factors which I believe play an even larger part in allowing a child with disabilities to grow up to become a valued, respected and equal member of the community.

Sadly, but understandably, there will always be a number of people who find it very difficult, if not impossible, to face and deal with disability of any kind, which means that there will always be situations where disabled children – and also adults, for that matter – find themselves excluded or ignored. In these instances the root of the problem lies with the other person rather than with the child – and there is little that can be done to rectify the situation other than a long process of education and familiarisation.

However, there are many other occasions where the child has difficulty in being accepted not because of his disabilities but because of his behaviour and attitude – both to others and to life in general. It is widely believed that such problems are an inevitable result of living with a disability, but this does not need to be so – and indeed social problems are frequently (although by no means always) the result of how the child has been raised and what has been expected of and accepted from him.

The subject of behaviour is dealt with later in the book but the aim of this chapter is to make parents aware of some of the traps they can unwittingly fall into, and to give them some ideas of steps they can take to help their child find the acceptance that should be his due. The points listed are in no particular order of priority and are by necessity very general in nature.

Don't underestimate your child

One basic mistake, common to many parents, is to assume that because their child has little or no understanding and an inability to communicate, he will not be likely, or even able, to learn how to manipulate them in the same way that children without disabilities do. Believing this will lead to untold problems for the family later in the child's life, by which time it will be very difficult to adopt a new approach to him. A disabled baby will learn just as quickly as any other that if someone picks him up whenever he cries, all he has to do is cry every time he is put down to guarantee being left there for a minimum of time. If he prefers Mum to feed him, all that is necessary to increase the chances of this happening is for him to go rigid and clamp his jaw shut tight every time somebody else tries. If he doesn't like being treated or exercised, screaming as though in pain or crying as though his heart will break is usually enough to bring the session to an early end.

Children are born manipulators and disabled children are no different in this respect, although their methods are often more subtle and can go un-noticed because adults tend to find it difficult to accept that "the poor little mite, with all his problems" could possibly be smart enough to control them. Children also have an ability to tune in to the moods of the adults around them, especially the ones who handle them on a regular basis, and are quick to learn which actions, expressions and sounds will consistently make Mum or Dad feel sorry for them or guilty about pushing them too hard, or will make them want to protect them from everything and everybody. In nearly all of these cases, the end product is the same – they will get their own way!

There is, of course, no real harm in occasionally allowing your child to manipulate you *as long as you are aware that this is what is happening* and are able to decide when it has gone on for long enough. However, accepting this as a permanent state of affairs will result in your child slowly but surely gaining control of all of your lives without you being fully aware of what is happening.

Discourage your child from becoming "clingy"

Nearly all young children go through a stage of not wanting Mummy to be out of sight, which can make life very difficult for a period of time. Most parents cope with this by insisting that he must be left for short periods with grandparents, aunties, friends or babysitters, knowing that eventually he will learn that his parents will always come back to him and so will accept their absence. (Also, anybody who has looked after other people's children on a regular basis will know that invariably within minutes of being left, the tears will stop and they will find something or somebody to happily occupy them!) Apart from cases where a child is exceptionally shy or insecure, this behaviour is only a temporary stage which he will gradually pass through.

With a disabled child, however, there is a very real danger that this "clingy" stage can become permanent, encouraged in a variety of ways without people realising it. First of all, although parents are reluctant to admit it, there is often a feeling that nobody else, however much they may care for the child, will be able to cope with him or interpret his wants and needs as well as they do, which makes them feel guilty about leaving him and stops them from enjoying their time away from him. Secondly, you will probably find that relatives and friends do not initially come forward and offer to look after your handicapped child, partly because they do not want to intrude or give the impression that they think you are unable to cope, partly because they are afraid that you will not trust *them* to be able to cope, and partly because until they have spent time handling the child and getting to know him they will be lacking confidence in their own abilities (unless, of course, they have prior experience with handicapped children). Thirdly, the child himself will very quickly respond to the emotions of all the people concerned – the guilt and doubts about leaving him experienced by his parents, the lack of confidence and uncertainty of those he is left with – and will learn to use them to his own advantage by playing on them and so creating a distressing situation for all concerned, which nobody is anxious to repeat more often than is necessary. The result is that the child is left with others so infrequently that he never really gets used to the idea, so each time is just as traumatic for everybody as the time before.

When your child is young it may not bother you unduly that you can't really leave him with people, but it is really not in anyone's interests – your own, his or other members of your family – to allow him to become totally dependent on you, if for no other reason than to safeguard against times of illness, stress or demands from other quarters which may force you to spend time away from him. Also, if he is to have the opportunity to grow and develop as a person in his own right he needs to learn that he does not have to rely on you for everything.

Encourage interaction with your child

The basis of social growth and development for all of us is the ability to interact with others at varying levels of function. It is therefore important that from a very early stage you try and set up situations where your child can respond to you and you to him. Initial responses are usually very simple in nature – holding eye contact, laughing when tickled, smiling at a funny noise, cooing and gurgling when spoken or sung to – and can only become more meaningful and sophisticated if they in turn generate a response from you. These simple two-way communications between adult and child quickly develop into little games and gradually the child learns to anticipate your probable response. This then encourages him to repeat actions, sounds, etc, which are likely to produce the reaction from you that pleases him most, and social interaction has thus begun.

Parents of a disabled baby, or of a child who has become disabled as a result of trauma, often find it difficult to play with him. Sometimes this is because the child doesn't respond as they expect him to, which in turn subdues their own reaction to him. Sometimes it is more a question that they feel awkward or embarrassed and don't know where to start. In some instances the parents are so overwhelmed by the child's problems that their primary emotions are sorrow, guilt and pity, which makes it very difficult to generate any sense of fun or enjoyment with the child.

However, by far the most common problem we see with parents is that they are so conscious of their child's disability that they are afraid of hurting or upsetting him, with the result that they 'wrap the child in cotton-wool' and in so doing deprive him of a lot of vital stimulation. All young children thrive on games of rough and tumble and love being swung up in the air, tossed around, tickled etc, and it is often during games of this nature that real contact is made with the parents and relationships begin to form. Your disabled child is not so fragile that he will break and he is no less capable of deriving great enjoyment from this kind of play – even if, on some occasions, it needs to be modified to give consideration to additional problems such as feeding tubes, a tendency to vomit, brittle bones etc – and it is very sad for all concerned if this element is missing from your lives.

Your child will not come to any harm as long as you handle him carefully, securely and with confidence and it could provide him with his first experience of real laughter.

You will also probably be surprised at how having fun with your child brings you closer and helps you to understand each other.

Introduce your child to different social situations

It is important that from very early on in his life you take your child into different places, settings and situations in order for him to learn how to adapt and feel at ease with change. Too many handicapped children can only function and behave under very specific conditions, in particular surroundings with particular people present. This often begins in a very low-key way, with the child simply seeming to be happiest when keeping to a very familiar routine. Of course, routine does play an important part in the life of all young children, but there is a fine line to be drawn before it crosses over to become rigidity, regimentation, or even obsession, and when this occurs the family can forget any semblance of normal life. They can never stay away from home as the child becomes unbearably miserable and cannot settle, let alone sleep. Their days will have no room for spontaneous changes of plan, since deviating from the usual agenda will produce a tantrum to end all tantrums. Nights out for parents become few and far between as their child is only prepared to be left with one person, and they don't like to impose too often.

Simply re-organising the furniture or changing the positions of a couple of items in a room can cause untold distress.

In many instances families settle for the option of an easy life and adapt their lifestyle to accommodate the child's desire for sameness. While this is, to some extent, understandable it is entirely the wrong approach, since over the years they will find that they have created a prison for the whole family which can only lead to frustration, resentment and general dissatisfaction for all concerned. If you can just persevere in the early days and cope with the tears, tantrums and lack of co-operation, your child will gradually learn that change does not have to pose a threat to his security and he may even grow to enjoy variety.

Help your child become aware of himself

If a child is going to be able to relate to others and interact with them, he first of all needs to be aware of himself as a person, and this is a concept that often does not come easily to a child with disabilities. We all have our own pre-conceived ideas of how he feels and his level of awareness of his problems, but unless he is extremely articulate with language it is impossible for us to really know. With some children it is difficult to be sure if they even know who they are or how they fit in to their family unit. Additionally, children with physical handicaps sometimes have difficulty in accepting that the affected parts of their bodies actually exist, so a child with paralysed legs cannot properly relate to the fact that his shoes are on *his* feet. Similarly, a child with perception problems may not be aware that his body has a front and a back – and so will be unaware of anything that is going on behind him. Taking all of this into account, it is no small wonder that a disabled child may not be able to identify with other children, as he may be finding it difficult to recognise the similarities between himself and them.

In order to increase your child's self awareness you should frequently draw his attention to parts of his body that lie outside the scope of his perception by touching, moving and, where possible, bringing them within his line of visibility. You should also make reference to his different emotional states, using words such as 'happy', 'sad', 'excited', 'fed-up', 'scared', etc, so that he can begin to identify his own moods and those of others around him. At the same time, however, you need to talk about his relationship to other members of the family, so that his awareness of himself does not develop in isolation and exclusion from everyone else.

I'm sure that by now some of you are thinking that your child's limitations are such that he could not possibly understand any of these words or concepts. The danger of underestimating his level of comprehension is dealt with in greater depth in the chapter relating to intellectual development, but it needs to be pointed out strongly here that *the only way children ever learn to understand language is by frequently hearing it used*. If the same things are said to him often enough, he will gradually start to make associations. In other words, *always speak to your child as though he is understanding you*. And remember that baby talk is strictly for babies! If you persist in using it with your child you can't blame others for treating him as a baby.

Encourage give-and-take

If your child is going to be accepted and integrated into society he must first of all be accepted by his peers, and for this to happen his behaviour needs to conform, to a large extent, to the group he is with, even if his abilities do not. Being possessive with his toys is acceptable as long as the children he is with are also at that stage of development, but any hope of an emerging friendship will be doomed at the start if he 'throws a wobbly' when those who understand the need to share show interest in what he is doing.

The question of give-and-take does not only apply to possessions and tangible items but also to people and time. To be a successful member of any group, your child needs to understand and accept that he cannot always be the centre of attention and that the others are not always going to do what he wants them to. He must also learn that the time and attention of any adult involved must be shared amongst all members of the group and is not his by right. On the same lines, things will not always automatically happen when he wants them to and there will be times when he has to patiently wait. Equally so, he must learn that there are occasions where it is necessary to take turns – such as when there is only one swing, or if a group of children are being shown something one at a time – and that he will have to wait until his turn comes around if he wants to take part.

All the points raised above do, of course, equally apply to the child as a member of the family unit. The temptation is always to give in to the child with disabilities as a way of compensating for his problems, but the result of this can only be that he grows up with an exaggerated sense of his own importance. In the years ahead it is important that he is valued and respected by the rest of the family for himself and the contribution he makes – and whereas a small child being the centre of attention can be seen as cute, an adult making those same demands is not so amusing. The outcome is usually that resentment builds up, nobody really wants to spend time with him and he becomes more isolated, which in turn makes him even more demanding on the occasions when he is in the company of others.

Teach your child to respect others

As well as developing self-awareness, it is important that your child is encouraged to take notice of and respect others. All young children are far more concerned with themselves, their own wants and needs, their own feelings and emotions, etc, than with what is happening to others around them. In most families it is usually the ups and downs of daily life that eventually teach the child that he is not the only one to be taken into consideration, that things that make him laugh actually upset his brother, that there is no point in screaming and shouting when Mummy is leaving him behind because it won't make her change her mind, that if he makes his little sister cry your attention and sympathy will be given to her, not him.

Your disabled child will not automatically develop a respect for other people; it is something he can only learn through example. If he knows that you always give the same consideration to the wishes of his brothers and sisters as to his own and that you are quick to sense when one of them is unhappy or unwell, he will himself start to become sensitive to the feelings of others and begin to understand how to moderate his behaviour to suit the situation. For example, that when Mummy is tired or worried is *not* the best time to refuse to eat and demanding attention when his brother is miserable or hurt is not likely to meet with success. Initially this awareness will be more closely related to how it affects him than to the wellbeing of the people concerned, but eventually it will grow into a real concern for and empathy with others.

As has already been pointed out, it is important that your disabled child does not develop the impression that he is more important or special to you than his brothers and sisters. Whilst it may be true that the nature of his problems make it necessary for you to spend more time with him or cause you more heartache or anguish, and whilst deep down you may be conscious of the fact that you are able to show more patience, tolerance and compassion for this child than your others, you must make sure that the child himself – or for that matter *any* of your children – are totally unaware of this. He must learn that your love, time and attention are equally shared by all of them and will be demonstrated to whichever one has the most pressing need at any given time. He should be in no doubt that if his actions or behaviour upset one of the other children and they retaliate, it is they and not he who will receive your sympathy and understanding and that you do not automatically take his side in squabbles and disagreements. He also needs to understand that you, his parents, have your own lives and interests, your own likes and dislikes, and that you do not always put his wishes before your own.

Don't lose sight of what is "normal"

As has been pointed out on numerous occasions throughout this book, it is only too easy (and understandable) for parents of a disabled child to see *every* little problem as being a result of his condition, whereas, in reality, a large proportion of them are due to nothing more than the fact that he is a child. Many of the social problems shown by a child with disabilities are no different from those shown by one without, other than the fact that they may be evident at a different age or stage of development.

We are all familiar with the "terrible twos" which can, in a split second, transform the most angelic child into a rigid, screaming dynamo of rage and, just as quickly, back into his usual sunny little self. Nobody is surprised when that same two-year-old refuses point-blank to let another child play with one of his toys, even though he himself until then has shown no interest in it. Similarly, it is accepted that although he insists on feeding himself you can guarantee that, despite his being provided with a spoon, the vast majority of food will reach his mouth via his fingers.

All of these characteristics are generally seen as being typical of a child of that age. Parents simply sigh and recall that their older children were just as impossible at the same age and look forward to a few months ahead when Junior has hopefully moved through that phase in his development.

However, if those very same characteristics are displayed by an eight-year-old disabled child, people are both horrified and embarrassed. Eight-year-olds are not supposed to throw temper tantrums; you should be able to reason with them. Children of that age should not be possessive; they should be prepared to share their toys. And surely a child of that age should have learned some table manners? What is often not taken into account is that although the child has lived for eight years, his development may have been slowed to the point that he has only reached the stage of a two-year-old, or that while he may be physically able his comprehension of language may be virtually non-existent – and how can you possibly reason with someone who doesn't understand your language? In other words, the behaviour you are witnessing may seem very out of place in a child of that age, but it is not necessarily *abnormal* when viewed in the context of his overall development.

6. Encouraging Self-Help

One of the most difficult things to recognise in a baby with disabilities is the appropriate time to start encouraging him to do things for himself.

When they see a small child struggling to do something, *every parent's instinct is to intervene and make life as easy as possible for him.* And when time is of the essence, you can't help thinking it would be quicker and easier to do it for him.

However, *it is not in the child's best interests to do this* and not expecting or allowing him to do things for himself will lead, at best, to a lack of motivation and, at worst, to the acquisition of a state of "learned helplessness".

Don't keep your child a baby

When there is a delay in either his physical or mental development, it is very easy to continue to think of your child as a baby and to treat him and talk to him as such. Only too often, I have seen four and five-year-olds who are still bottle-fed, not because they can't cope with cups and spoons but because either it is faster or the parents have simply got into the habit of giving a bottle and have not thought to try any other means. Similarly, a child who can quite clearly understand much of what is being said to him might still be spoken to in 'baby talk'.

Always try to keep your child's actual age in mind and look for areas where he might be able to cope with experiences and opportunities relevant to children of that age. Even if physically he is still at the stage of a young baby, unable to sit or move around, he might understand enough to be able to at least assist you with dressing, feeding, etc. If, on the other hand, he is physically able and active but with little comprehension, you might still be able to teach him to do things for himself by repeatedly showing him and taking him through the motions.

In other words, *your child's disabilities do not mean that you must always do everything for him.*

Establish proper sleeping and waking times

The first few weeks of any baby's life are spent feeding and sleeping, with occasional spells of wakefulness. As he develops awareness of his surroundings and starts to respond to people, these periods of being awake become longer, with definite nap times which gradually become shorter. By the middle of the second year, most active toddlers can get by with an afternoon nap – and indeed many parents will strive to keep them awake during the day to ensure an unbroken night's sleep. By the age of three it is not uncommon for children to have discarded sleeping in the day altogether, other than when they are not well or have been extremely busy.

When a baby's development is delayed, however, either physically or mentally, there is a tendency for long daytime naps to continue way beyond the age of other children. This is often for no other reason than that there is little close-by of interest to him or that he is unable to move around to explore his environment. In the absence of stimulation he simply becomes bored and falls asleep.

These frequent naps, together with the fact that he is using little or no energy when he is awake, will often result in him being awake more at night, indeed, his sleep pattern at night will probably be similar to that during the day, in that he is taking short naps rather than sleeping for longer periods of time.

This is potentially the beginning of a vicious circle. Because he is seldom awake and active for long, he never gets really tired, so he doesn't go into a deep and restful sleep, then, because he is only taking naps, he never wakes properly refreshed, so he always dozy when he is awake.

The end product is a baby who fluctuates between half asleep and half awake, a state which is not conducive to either taking in information from or responding to his environment and those around him.

To avoid falling into this trap, from an early age try to set specific periods of time for playing with him, stimulating his senses and moving him around, so that he has no option but to stay awake.

If you are working in another room, take him with you, placing him in a baby chair or bouncy cradle where he can see you, and keep on talking to him. When you sense he might be getting tired, put him in his cot and darken the room – this will help to establish a definite place for sleeping and will discourage him from drifting off to sleep wherever he happens to be.

Take this opportunity to get on with any chores you might have to do, so that when he wakes up you can spend time playing and talking to him again.

Don't fall into the trap of leaving him to sleep for hours on end. Although it might be convenient for you to have time without interruption to get on with things, it really won't help the situation. If, after an hour or so, he is showing no signs of stirring, wake him up, then keep him moving until he is fully awake, otherwise he is likely to just drift back. We all know how easy it is to do that after being woken by the alarm clock; babies are no exception.

Never allow him to miss a meal because he wants to sleep; that will only result in all meal times being pushed back so that you are feeding him much later, which in turn will make it harder for him to settle.

If your baby wakes frequently in the night, try to establish routines that encourage him to go back to sleep. Don't get him up and play with him, he will think that night and day are the same. Keep the room as dark as possible, use a night light if necessary rather than turning on the overhead light, and whenever possible soothe him by stroking and talking softly rather than picking him up.

He will gradually learn that lying somewhere dark and quiet means sleep, while being moved around with lots to see means being awake.

Once good sleep routines are established you will see a marked difference in the quality of your baby's waking hours as well as in his responsiveness.

Push the pace with feeding

As has already been mentioned, many children with disabilities remain on liquid diets for much longer than is either necessary or desirable. There seem to be a number of common reasons for this: a failure to recognise that the child is developing beyond the baby stage, a fear that he will be unable to cope with solid food and might choke, the fact that giving a bottle is faster and more convenient or a lack of interest in food on the part of the child himself.

It is most important that the child is weaned onto solid food as close to the relevant age as possible. His growing body needs more nutrients than those provided in milk alone, both for his organs to function properly and for him to develop stamina. He needs a variety of tastes, textures and smells to stimulate his senses and, last but not least, the actions of chewing and swallowing will help develop the control of his mouth, throat and breathing that will be necessary for him to learn to speak.

When you first start spoon-feeding your child, experiment with positions until you find one which suits you both. Some parents prefer to hold the child on their lap, supporting his head in the crook of their arm, while others are happier putting him into a seat or propping him on cushions. Try and stay as relaxed as possible – only too often feeding becomes a battleground, with Mum's tension and the child's distress rising in equal proportions.

One of the key factors in spoon-feeding solids is getting the timing right. If the child has recently been given a bottle, he won't be hungry, so the food offered will be of little interest. If he is desperately hungry he will want instant satisfaction and will only recognise the bottle as the means of providing this. Offering a snack halfway between normal feeding times is therefore often the best solution.

The first food you try should be very smooth, thicker than milk, so it doesn't just run out or slip straight down and make him choke, and quite bland in taste. Remember that, until now, he has only tasted milk and anything with a strong flavour will be a shock to him. Fruit-flavoured yoghurt or mashed potato with gravy are good starting points and will give a contrast between slightly sweet and slightly savoury.

Use a soft spoon and hold it just inside his mouth, allowing him initially to suck from the spoon, and talk gently to him to give him reassurance. Don't be put off if he pulls a face, wriggles or spits it out, these are all quite usual reactions from any baby starting with solids.

If he has difficulty swallowing the food or it comes straight back out, try depositing it in different places within his mouth – on the tongue, against the roof of the mouth, at the side – until you find a system that works for both of you. There are no hard and fast rules, it will depend on the child's particular disability and his own preferences.

Keep going for at least four or five spoonfuls and don't offer the bottle immediately afterwards, especially if the session has not gone particularly well – all he will learn is that you desperately want him to have food and if he refuses he will be given his bottle.

Once you have started to offer solids, do this on a regular basis, once or twice a day, until he is comfortable with it, then introduce them as part of regular meal times before each bottle, gradually widening the variety of tastes and increasing the amount of food, with a corresponding reduction in the volume of milk. Replace daytime bottles with a training cup and, eventually, a normal cup, both of which will help to move away from the perception of him as a baby.

As soon as your child is happily eating solid food, start to introduce different textures and lumps, by mashing or chopping the food rather than pureeing or blending. Remember that older babies and toddlers like to try finger foods – rusks, bread, cheese, banana – which may not be accessible to your child if he has little hand function, so break off small pieces for him and put them into his mouth. If you are eating something different to him, offer him a taste, even if it has a strong flavour – you might be surprised by his developing tastebuds.

Finally, don't let feeding and meal times become an issue or a means of emotional blackmail. Children will eat when they are hungry and unless he is significantly underweight he won't come to any harm if he misses a meal or two. Don't let him think that getting him to eat is a matter of primary importance to you as this will only create conflict; a 'take it or leave it' approach will have far more chance of success.

The question of toilet training

Many parents mistakenly feel that it is not possible for a child who is unable to communicate his needs to become toilet trained but, in my experience, this does not have to be the case.

To be successful, toilet training must be low-key but, at the same time, consistent. It is not fair to your child to expect him to understand that on some days you will be very enthusiastic about it and want him to 'perform to order', while on others you will be quite happy for him to wet his nappy because toilet training is not convenient to your schedule. Too many parents get uptight about it, stop and start, and then give up because it is not worth the hassle. All the child learns from this is that there are no set rules, so it is too difficult for him to comprehend what is expected of him.

A number of factors need to taken into consideration when starting a programme of toilet training, each of equal importance, and they are listed below.

❖ You must be serious about wanting to tackle the problem; it is not something you can play at or do half-heartedly.

❖ You must have a suitable potty or toilet adaption which allows your child to feel secure and is also easy for you in respect of handling.

❖ Once you start, your child should be taken out of nappies during the day at all times – so be prepared for some accidents!

❖ Nothing will be achieved by making your child sit on the potty for long periods in the hope that he will eventually perform – he will very quickly lose concentration and forget why he is there. The maximum time he should ever be left there without a result is two minutes.

❖ The real key to success lies in giving your child frequent opportunity to use the potty, and I would suggest that you take him every half hour throughout the day. The only way he can possibly learn control is if he knows that when he feels he wants to go, he won't have to wait long before he is given the chance. If he has no idea of when he will next be taken, he will not even attempt to hold on.

❖ If your child fails to perform, don't make too much fuss, just comment that he obviously didn't want to go and that you will take him again soon. On the other hand, if you get the desired result, be very generous with your praise, so he realises that he has achieved what you wanted.

❖ When you have reached the stage that you are having very few "accidents", you should start to gradually extend the times between visits to the loo, so that your child slowly gains greater control.

With a little patience and determination, toilet training can be achieved with a minimum of fuss, and the benefits to both your child and yourselves are worth the effort involved.

Obviously, in some cases it may prove to be more a question that you have become more tuned-in to your child and have trained yourself to behave consistently so that you are able to "catch" him, rather than that he understands what is happening – but the end result is effectively the same.

Motivation and a sense of achievement

As babies grow into toddlers and start to assert themselves, they develop an overwhelming sense of independence, which often makes them want to try to do things which are way beyond their capability or comprehension. Many parents experience the frustration of a child who insists that they want to do it themselves – whether it be dressing, feeding, or getting a toy to work – when it is clear that it is not going to be possible and will result in the inevitable temper tantrum when the child realises that he cannot, in fact, perform the task.

However, a little patience from the parent, together with subtle intervention and assistance, usually results in successful completion, for which the child is rewarded by the satisfaction of achievement accompanied by the praise of the adult. This is all part of the continuing learning process and encourages the child to keep on trying and developing new skills.

The slower development of a child with a disability, however, often means that opportunities for encouraging independence are overlooked, even though the child might be longing to try to do something himself. If he can't convey this desire to his parents, they will probably automatically perform the task for him without a second thought, simply because it hasn't occurred to them that he might want to try. However, it is a fact of life that if things are always done for us, we eventually lose the motivation to even try to do them for ourselves, and disabled children are no exception, especially if what they are trying to achieve requires great effort and their attempts go unrecognised.

Encourage your child whenever possible to at least 'have a go' – helping him where necessary – and be sure to give lots of praise for his efforts. Show him that you expect him to be doing some things for himself and only offer help after he has made a visible effort.

Of course, he will often fail, but as long as he is not made to feel inadequate by his failure and you are there to help him complete the task, he will not be put off, and will learn that being prepared to try is, in itself, an achievement.

Only with continual encouragement and recognition of his efforts and achievements will he acquire the self-motivation that is vital for his ultimate development of independence.

Recognise and avoid "learned helplessness"

There is a fine line between a child, or indeed an adult, who genuinely cannot do something and one who has learned that it is in his best interests to act as if he can't – and it is often extremely difficult to recognise the difference.

If you are honest with yourself, you will have to admit that there have been many occasions when you have utilised a form of *learned helplessness* yourself in order to get somebody else to do something that you are quite capable of doing yourself but would rather not have to do. An example of this, for a woman, might be changing a light bulb or checking the oil in the car, or in the case of a man it might be ironing a shirt or cooking a meal.

We often use the "I can't do it as well as you" excuse when faced with a task that we know we could perform ourselves but don't want to because it requires too much effort – and why should we, if somebody else is prepared to do it for us?

Children – including those with disabilities – are no exception to this and are often more astute than adults at recognising situations where they can put it to use. Many parents express surprise when told that their child uses a spoon quite happily at nursery when they are continuing to feed him at home, or that he is capable of getting himself from one place to another when they are still carrying him everywhere – and in many cases it is not so much the fact that the child doesn't *want* to do these things for himself at home, he simply realises that by *not* doing them the end product will be more individual time and contact with Mum or Dad.

You can encourage him to do more for himself if you show him that you are not abandoning him to fend for himself. You will still be there with him, but will be spending the time giving him encouragement and praise, rather than doing everything for him. Slowly, he will learn that he can derive more satisfaction and pleasure from his own achievements and your appreciation of them than from having you do things for him.

There is, of course, nothing at all wrong with sometimes doing things for your child that you know he is able to do himself, as long as you make it clear that you are doing them because, on that occasion, you want to and it suits you, and not because he is making you feel that he can't or that it's too difficult for him. We all like to be 'spoiled' from time to time – just make sure he is aware of it and appreciates it.

Independence – the ultimate goal

For any parent of a child with a disability, the ultimate goal has to be that he can live as independently as possible. This does not mean that he has to be perfect, or to attain high academic standards or be able to engage in public speaking. It doesn't *even* mean that he can live alone and look after himself. What it does mean is that, within his level of ability, whatever that might be, he is able to make choices, show his preferences, communicate his needs to others and have some influence over the quality of his own life.

At the top end of the scale, this might involve living in his own house, either alone or with a partner, holding down a good job and enjoying a full and active social life.

At the lower end it might mean having a say in the environment in which he is cared for, who will care for him and having some control over his day-to-day activities and basic needs.

For most, it will be somewhere in between these two extremes.

The most we can hope for with any of our children, with or without disability, is that they are happy and getting the most they possibly can from life, that they are respectful of others and respected themselves for who they are.

There is no *blueprint* for parenting; all any of us can do is try our best to give our children the means to succeed to the best of their individual abilities.

7. Encouraging Good Behaviour

If you are the parents of a young disabled baby, you are probably wondering what relevance this chapter holds for you because your child isn't old enough or able enough to be exhibiting 'behaviour' of any kind, either good or bad. However, my aim here is to help you to recognise the beginnings of undesirable behaviour patterns and to give you some ideas of how best to deal with them.

A child growing up with a disability is already at a disadvantage in that strangers, whether adults or other children, will at first be wary of how to approach and respond to him, purely through a lack of understanding of the disability itself. This disadvantage will be compounded if the child behaves in a way which surprises or even shocks onlookers but this behaviour seems to go unnoticed or unchecked by the parents themselves.

Children wouldn't be children if they behaved perfectly all the time, nor would we want or expect them to, but we still hope that when the situation requires them to behave well, they won't 'show us up' or 'let us down'.

Many parents of disabled children feel that they have enough to contend with in simply trying to overcome their child's difficulties; wondering whether the child's behaviour is perceived as 'good' or 'bad' is the last thing on their minds. Indeed, in some instances they feel that this is an unavoidable consequence of his disability, just another thing they must learn to cope with, but one that does not rate highly in the general scheme of things.

However, the whole issue of behaviour and how it is dealt with might affect and influence the lives of the whole family, not least the disabled child himself.

Understanding the need

Something that will quickly single your child out from others is if his behaviour is not appropriate to what is happening, such as laughing when he is hurt or told off, shouting and running around when others are sitting down watching television or listening to a story, or picking up an item to look at it closely then suddenly losing interest and throwing it onto the floor before wandering off to investigate something else. However, it will not only be his actions and behaviour that draw attention to him, but also the way in which the adults around him deal with it.

If, to the casual observer, what looks to be simply the antics of a 'naughty' child go unchecked and apparently un-noticed by the accompanying adults, you can expect to be the object of disapproving looks. If you are at a public event and you allow your child to spoil the enjoyment of other people by running around, knocking into people and making a noise, don't expect him to be shown understanding and compassion. If your child is allowed to snatch things from other children and always get his own way, don't be surprised if parents are reluctant to encourage their children to play with him. However, if on occasions like this you are seen to be aware that his behaviour is inappropriate to the situation and to be making an effort to show him what is expected of him, you will find people far more willing to accept and encourage him.

Sadly, it is only too easy for a disabled child to grow up believing that he does not have to conform to the codes of behaviour that apply to other children, that he can 'get away with anything', that his parents will always make allowances for him and that he never has to face the consequences of his behaviour.

As well as being in the child's best interests, encouraging good behaviour will also bring benefits to other members of the family, who might have found that they too have been excluded from invitations to social occasions for fear that they might have the badly behaved child in tow. Additionally, in the long run, a child who 'understands the rules' is generally happier and easier to live with.

What is good behaviour?

Generally speaking, the image of a well-behaved child is one whose actions are appropriate to whatever situation he is in, who listens to his parents, who isn't loud or unruly, who is neither selfish nor spiteful and who shows respect for other people and their possessions.

In reality, though, while every family has its own standards of what is acceptable, most of us would settle for a child who doesn't show us up in public, attract negative attention, spoil the enjoyment of others or blatantly disobey instructions.

There are several points to take into consideration when trying to encourage and teach your disabled child to behave well:

1. Children are not born with an inbuilt understanding of the difference between good and bad behaviour;

2. How you react to their behaviour has a strong influence on how it develops;

3. Children won't behave well just because you *tell* them to – they have to learn that it is *in their own interests* to do so

and that their behaviour has consequences they can, to some extent, control;

4. Children crave attention and will go to any lengths to get it – but if they cannot get positive attention from the adults around them they will settle for negative!

Moulding behaviour

As babies become toddlers and start to explore their surroundings, we start to mould their behaviour with the use of simple terms such as "no", "don't touch", "put it down" or "good boy", "clever boy" and "well done". When accompanied by the appropriate tone of voice and facial expression, this is usually sufficient to modify and reinforce the child's actions as they try to elicit a positive response from you. If this fails, the next intuitive step is usually distraction – drawing the child's interest to something else and thus removing the focus of negative behaviour. It is very rare at this stage to hear a young toddler described as 'naughty' or 'badly behaved'.

As the child develops intelligence, personality and intention the subject of behaviour – and in particular how to encourage the right kind of behaviour – becomes more complex. The more a child understands, the more they will question, either verbally or by their actions and behaviour. They will also go through a stage of trying to establish control over situations they are in and over the adults surrounding them and it is important that they are reminded, by both words and actions, that it is, in fact, the parents who have the final say. Possessiveness and selfishness are common attributes of the young child, which sadly can continue through life unless an adult steps in to show that by sharing with others the child will also benefit by being granted access to what the others have.

Sometimes parents feel guilty if they are continually checking their child or stopping him from doing things, but in truth children generally like to understand the rules and to know the limits that have been set for them. The only way they can accomplish this is by watching the reactions of the adults around them to how they are behaving.

Consistency is the key

The more consistent the reactions of the adults, the faster a child will learn to modify how he behaves in particular situations. If the response from adults is inconsistent or vague, however, the child will continually push to see how far the boundaries can be extended. If, on some occasions, he is told off for behaving in a certain way but at other times the same behaviour is ignored or even condoned, the child becomes confused and will often keep repeating that same behaviour in an attempt to find out what the adults really mean.

An example of this is a child who keeps getting out of bed in the middle of the night and nine times out of ten is taken straight back, but on the tenth occasion the parents can't be bothered and let him stay up for another hour. Do you think the child will remember the nine times he was put back into his bed or the once when he was allowed an extra hour of playing? He knows that it worked once, so now he will try to make it happen again – even if it takes 100 times!

Try also to be consistent with your responses, regardless of who else might be present. Some parents who, in the privacy of their own home, would have no qualms about disciplining a child for, say, being too noisy, might find it difficult to reprimand the exact same behaviour if other people are present and will simply ignore the boisterous child with an apologetic smile, perhaps because they are embarrassed or because they are afraid that others might judge their rebuke too harsh.

Conversely, if their child hits out at another, they might sharply reprimand him in public, in order to be seen as 'taking control of the situation', whereas if he did the same thing at home to one of his siblings, or even a parent, they might let it go unchecked with the excuse "he doesn't understand" or "he didn't mean to hurt you".

Of course, the lesson the child learns from either of these situations is that if he chooses the right time and place, he can get away with behaving badly.

It is also important to maintain consistency among the adults who are closely involved with the child. It is pointless Dad taking toys from him because he is throwing them at people if Mum then gives them back to him, or if Mum says he can't have chocolate since he didn't eat his dinner only to find Grandma feeding it to him when she isn't looking.

What the child will learn from this is how to play one adult off against another and that every rule can be broken by this technique, so it's important to make all the family members aware of how you propose to handle different situations and aspects of behaviour and why. Ask for their co-operation and reassure them that there will be ample opportunities for rewarding good behaviour and that you will really appreciate their support.

Giving the right attention

The attention received from adults plays a big part in how a child will behave. We are all guilty of paying more attention to a child who is whining, crying or behaving badly, because these actions bring them to the forefront of our consciousness and demand some sort of response from us. If, on the other hand, the child is playing quietly or watching television, we take the opportunity of getting on with chores, reading or catching up with some hobby, usually doing no more than from time to time popping in to check that the child is OK.

When the child becomes restless or bored – as inevitably he will – and comes looking for company or distraction, we will probably be well into whatever we are doing and the chances are we will simply tell him to go and play. This, of course, is not what he wants, he wants attention, which he sees will not be forthcoming. This is usually when the whining starts and already he is starting to get what he is after, because how long can you listen to it without telling him to stop? This leads to more whining, at which point you will try and think of some distraction. "Why don't you go and get your crayons" or "go and put a video on". Either of these things he would be more than happy to do with you, but not alone, so he starts to cry, at which point you start to get cross and raise your voice. He might now stamp out of the room and you think you have won and that he has gone back to what he was doing – until you go in 10 minutes later and find that he has drawn on the wall or cut off all his hair. Your response to this will be entirely predictable – but guess what? – he certainly has 100 percent of your attention now, even if it results in tears and punishment!

I would be very surprised if any parent hasn't encountered something along these lines at some point.

Even the most severely disabled children are no different when it comes to wanting attention and, sadly, those most severely affected often fall victim to losing out simply because they are not in a position to demand it. If your child is unable to move around and can't vocalise what he wants, the chances are that you will settle him somewhere safe and comfortable, with things close by to stimulate him, then, while he is quiet, go and get on with something you need to do. If, after a while, he cries, you will most probably go to him and either pick him up or do something to entertain him, being quite prepared to spend some time with him.

If you think about it, what you have actually done is show him that crying – which might later in his life be seen as negative behaviour – brings the reward of your attention and time. It would be far better to make the effort to stay with him and amuse him while he is quiet and happy, then, after a while, to tell him that you are going out of the room to do something but you are leaving him with toys and maybe the television and will be back soon. If he is quiet, pop in frequently and tell him he is being a good boy and that you won't be long, but if he kicks up a fuss tell him firmly that you are busy and that he is fine with plenty of things to entertain him. Make sure now that you don't go back in while he is crying, wait until there is a lull, even if you suspect it is only temporary and say, "See, you didn't need to cry, I came back anyway."

You will undoubtedly notice your child's bad behaviour because you find it annoying or embarrassing, but you might be less tuned in to his good behaviour. If things are going nicely and all is quiet we tend to leave well alone! Remember that he wants your attention – whether it is negative or positive doesn't really matter – and if behaving well fails to attract attention he will revert to being naughty. Make sure he knows you have noticed when he is being good, even if only by saying "You're a good boy, you haven't moaned or been naughty all morning. That's really good, I'm going to give you a hug."

Choose rewards carefully

If you have decided that you are going to use a system of rewarding your child for behaving well, you need to think very carefully about what you are going to offer. This isn't about what *you* would like your child to have or do, it is purely about what *he* would find fun, exciting or motivational – for instance, offering an outing to a restaurant to a child who hates public places or is a fussy eater could turn out to be more of a punishment than a reward, and a new book for a child who prefers television is likely to be disregarded. In both cases, the fact that these "treats" have been earned by the child being on best behaviour will be completely lost.

Also, you should never make a reward out of something that is going to happen anyway, irrespective of how the child behaves – for instance, telling him you will take him swimming if he behaves well on a shopping trip is pointless if you have already promised your other child that you will go, because unless you have someone you can leave him with, he knows he will be going with you anyway, even if his behaviour in the shops is a nightmare.

In the same way, if you are thinking of depriving your child of something he enjoys as a consequence of him behaving in an unacceptable way, you should make sure that you are not inadvertently giving him what will be perceived as a reward, as the alternative might be more attractive than the "treat" they are missing out on. Being left behind with Grandma and having her undivided attention could well be seen as more exciting than the swimming he has missed and might encourage him to try for the same result next time.

The same rules for all the family

It is really important, not only for your disabled child but for others in the family, that the same rules apply to all of them, albeit that some might have to be modified to cater for specific problems.

As has already been pointed out, brothers and sisters can be hurt and resentful if they feel that you are not as strict with the one with disabilities and that you let him get away with more, often seeing this as a sign of favouritism.

Additionally, the disabled child himself will adopt the view that rules are only for others and don't apply to him.

One example of this is allowing to him to wander around the room eating his food when all the others have been made to sit at the table until they have finished – something which might seem small and insignificant to you but which might assume a greater importance to those involved.

This is easily remedied by fastening the child into a highchair, even if it means a few noisy and disruptive meal times. As long as you ignore this behaviour he will eventually stop.

Similarly, bedtime is usually a point of great contention with all siblings – the question of who gets to stay up later and why.

Don't fall into the trap of letting the child with disabilities be the last to go to bed just because it makes life easier for you, or at the very least make sure you give good reasons for doing this.

IN SUMMARY

Your child needs to learn the difference between good and bad behaviour, to know that he doesn't have to behave badly in order to get attention from you, that bad behaviour does not bring attention and to understand that you mean what you say and that both parents are following the same system, so he can't get a reward from one when it has been denied by the other.

At the same time, you need to learn to look for and acknowledge good behaviour, to not give more attention to bad behaviour than good, to be 100% consistent and to choose rewards carefully and make sure you can uphold them.

Remember that once he knows the rules, your child will settle down, but until then *every* day will be a challenge while he tests you to see how far you will let him go today.

As has been said elsewhere in this book, it is one thing for a child to be excluded because of his disability, which unfortunately is largely due to the ignorance of others, in which case little can be done to change the situation, but it is quite another thing if the exclusion is mainly due to behaviour which the people he comes into contact with find difficult to understand, accept or deal with.

To me this is inexcusable and totally unnecessary. It is the responsibility of parents and other family members to do their utmost to ensure that a disabled child has a basic understanding of what is acceptable and what is not.

There is always a danger that their disability will become an excuse for letting the child do whatever he wishes, as was highlighted on one memorable occasion when I heard a young boy who had been reprimanded by his mother respond with the statement, "You can't shout at me, I'm handicapped!"

If that is how he sees himself and his position in society, can we really blame others for having a negative attitude towards him?

A FINAL MESSAGE

I don't, for one moment, expect that I have solved any of your problems, taken away any of the pain or made the prospect of raising a child with disabilities something to look forward to.

What I do sincerely hope is that I have helped in some small way to guide you through the early stages of trying to focus on the problem and that I have offered some useful suggestions which might make your day-to-day life more manageable.

My greatest wish, though, is that I might have helped at least some of you to see beyond the problems and issues associated with disability and to appreciate the character and value of the special little person you have created.

USEFUL CONTACTS

Developmental Intervention
PO Box 62
Ammanford
Carms SA18 1WX
UK
www.developmentalintervention.co.uk

Catch Japan
Daishoju-cho 353-1
Isesaki-shi
Gunma-ken 372-0841
Japan
www2u.biglobe.ne.jp/~catch

The Willem Group
The Australian Institute for the Achievement of Human
Potential
PO Box 248
Mount Eliza
Victoria 3930
Australia
www.aiahp.org